What to Do
TILL JESUS COMES

"Behold, He is coming with the clouds."

by
Knofel Staton

You may obtain a 64-page leader's guide to accompany this paperback. Order number 41017 from Standard Publishing or your local supplier.

A Division of Standard Publishing
Cincinnati, Ohio 45231
No. 41016

All Scripture references are taken from *The New International Version,* © 1973 by New York Bible Society International, used by permission.

Library of Congress Cataloging in Publication Data

Staton, Knofel.
  What to do till Jesus comes.

  Summary: Discusses the concept of the return of Jesus and its implications for Christian life.
  1. Second Advent. [1. Second Advent. 2. Jesus Christ. 3. Christian life]   I. Title.
BT886.S65   236   81-14594
ISBN 0-87239-481-6   AACR 2

Printed in U.S.A.   1982

DEDICATION

This book is dedicated to two people who gave me the best they had—their daughter, Julia. To my in-laws—Ralph and Helen Coons.

IN APPRECIATION

I am deeply grateful to four people without whom this book would not have been written—My wife, Julia, who typed the first draft from my handwriting and served as my first editor; Jeaneane Chaney and Marilyn Smith, who typed the final copy; and Orrin Root, who asked me to write the book and who made valuable suggestions for the final product.

TABLE OF
CONTENTS

He *Is* Coming Back!

I thought the time would never come that I would be old enough to get my driver's license. But it did. I thought the time would never come that I would have a date. But it did. Then I thought the time would never come when that first date would end. But it did (thank goodness). I thought the time would never come for me to graduate from high school. But it did. I was so excited that I left my diploma on the seat in the auditorium. I had only one thought that night—"I'm done with education forever!"

I thought the time would never come for me to leave the military service. But it did. I thought the time would never come that I would have gray hair. But, alas, that time is here. I thought the time for me to wear bifocals would never happen. But that has happened also.

There have been days when I thought the time would never come for Jesus to return. I have thought that on occasion because basically I am an impatient person. I want what's coming to me tomorrow to happen yesterday. I want to get my clothes back from the cleaners before I have taken them in. If one person is in line ahead of me, I get this feeling that it will never be my turn. I would love to have a gadget in the car so that I could press a button and all the red lights at the intersections would turn green as I approached.

Don't be too harsh with me. There are many others like me in this country. If I had been born in another country, I might not even own a watch. And I probably would not be calling the "time and temperature" every morning. In another country, I might even take an afternoon siesta. I could take my time getting somewhere. I could walk or ride a horse or ride in a wagon. I might even stay and visit for two or three hours during a church meeting, instead of wondering if the preacher had a heart attack when it is one minute past ten and he is not on the platform yet.

Yes, we Americans are impatient. We are used to instant potatoes, instant coffee, instant tea, T.V. dinners, microwave ovens, remote control television, and even instant starters on our cars. We don't use calendars nearly as much as we use watches with second hands. Being late is considered to be poor etiquette here, while in some countries it is expected and customary. Procrastination is almost the unpardonable sin to us Americans. This constant pressure may explain why many Americans live on tranquilizers (two tons every day). If anyone has to wait, he pops a pill to calm him down.

It is little wonder that many Americans think Jesus will never return. After all, it already has been nearly two thousand years since He promised to come back!

Christians began to wonder about the "slowness" of Jesus' return even before all the apostles had died. (We Americans did not invent impatience; we have just perfected it.) The impatient scoffers in the first century were vocal: "Where is this 'coming' he promised? Ever since our fathers died, everything goes on as it has since the beginning of creation" (2 Peter 3:4).

How wrong they were! Things have never been a mere repeat of preceding days. Some people think that today, but they easily forget about carrying in the coal, using ice boxes instead of refrigerators, milking the cow, carrying in water from the well, using the party line on the phone so that nothing was a secret, and getting out of bed on a cold morning to step on icy linoleum.

Peter reminded the scoffers that things had changed for them also: "But they deliberately forget that long ago by God's word the heavens existed and the earth was formed out of water and with water. By water also the world of that time was deluged and destroyed. By the same word the present heavens and earth are reserved for fire, being kept for the day of judgment and destruction of ungodly men (2 Peter 3:5-7). Peter reminded them that God is in control. God will decide when to stop time. Peter also reminded them that God is a patient God who keeps His promises.

God's Patience

We may be tempted to question God's promise of Jesus' return if we use the wrong kind of instrument to measure the passing of time. When we watch a clock that ticks off minutes and seconds, time creeps. The less active we are, the slower time seems to pass. If you think Jesus is taking too long to return, chances are you are not active enough working for Him. Active, working Christians do not even notice the "slowness." That is probably why we have so much Biblical teaching about remaining active until Jesus returns.

God existed before time was created, and He is going to continue to exist after time ceases. So God is not restricted by time. Time will never "run out" on Him. And He is in no hurry. He has all the time in the world because He owns time and controls it.

"The Lord is not slow in keeping His promise, as some understand slowness" (2 Peter 3:9). We understand slowness by our Timex or Bulova, but God does not. "With the Lord a day is like a thousand years, and a thousand years are like a day" (2 Peter 3:8). If a thousand years are like a day, only two days have passed since Jesus walked in Palestine. It is not even sunset on the second day yet. If we count time as God does, He is not slow in keeping His promise.

Peter was not saying that we should calculate God's haste or slowness. The delay in Christ's coming is not to be explained in God's slowness. It is not to be measured by minutes of the day, but by the mercy of the Deity. "He is patient with you, not wanting anyone to perish, but everyone to come to repentance" (2 Peter 3:9). Aren't you glad Jesus did not come before you became a Christian? Then don't be impatient for Him to come back before others have the opportunity to become Christians. After all, He does not have to come back in your lifetime for you to receive eternal life. You can have eternal life in Jesus today.

God's Promises

Does this mean that Jesus will never return? No. He *will* return. Peter immediately made that point clear, "But the day of the Lord will come . . ." (2 Peter 3:10).

Every book in the New Testament except Philemon and 3 John speaks about the second coming of Jesus. It was implied in Philemon when Paul said that Philemon could have Onesimus back "for good" (Philemon 15). "For good" implies life beyond the second coming.

Here is a partial listing of the promises concerning the second coming. Some of them do not use the word *coming,* but you can see that they refer to that time.

For the Son of Man is going to come in his Father's glory (Matthew 16:27).

And you will see the Son of Man sitting at the right hand of the Mighty One and coming on the clouds of heaven (Mark 14:62).

10

You also must be ready, because the Son of Man will come at an hour when you do not expect him (Luke 12:40).

And if I go and prepare a place for you, I will come back and take you to be with me that you also may be where I am (John 14:3).

This same Jesus, who has been taken from you into heaven, will come back in the same way you have seen him go into heaven (Acts 1:11).

When he comes . . . then the end will come, when he hands over the kingdom to God the Father (1 Corinthians 15:23, 24).

We will boast of you in the day of the Lord Jesus (2 Corinthians 1:14).

Let us not become weary in doing good, for at the proper time we will reap a harvest if we do not give up (Galatians 6:9).

Having believed, you were marked in him with a seal, the promised Holy Spirit, who is a deposit guaranteeing our inheritance until the redemption of those who are God's possession—to the praise of his glory (Ephesians 1:13, 14).

But our citizenship is in heaven. And we eagerly await a Savior from there, the Lord Jesus Christ, who . . . will transform our lowly bodies so that they will be like his glorious body (Philippians 3:20, 21).

When Christ, who is your life, appears, then you also will appear with him in glory (Colossians 3:4).

For the Lord himself will come down from heaven, with a loud command, with the voice of the archangel and with the trumpet call of God, and the dead in Christ will rise first (1 Thessalonians 4:16).

God is just: He will pay back trouble to those who trouble you. . . . This will happen when the Lord Jesus is revealed from heaven in blazing fire with his powerful angels (2 Thessalonians 1:6, 7).

I charge you to keep this commandment without spot or blame until the appearing of our Lord Jesus Christ, which God will bring about in his own time (1 Timothy 6:13-15).

Now there is in store for me the crown of righteousness, which the Lord, the righteous Judge, will award to me on that day—and not only to me, but also to all who have longed for his appearing (2 Timothy 4:8).

It teaches us to say "No" to ungodliness and worldly passions, and to live self-controlled, upright and godly lives in this present age, while we wait for the blessed hope—the glorious appearing of our great God and Savior, Jesus Christ (Titus 2:12, 13).

And let us consider how we may spur one another on toward love and good deeds. Let us not give up meeting together, as some are in the habit of doing, but let us encourage one another—and all the more as you see the Day approaching (Hebrews 10:24, 25).

Be patient, then, brothers, until the Lord's coming (James 5:7).

12

Therefore, prepare your minds for action; be self-controlled; set your hope fully on the grace to be given you when Jesus Christ is revealed (1 Peter 1:13).

But in keeping with his promise we are looking forward to a new heaven and a new earth, the home of righteousness (2 Peter 3:13).

And now, dear children, continue in him, so that when he appears we may be confident and unashamed before him at his coming (1 John 2:28).

Watch out that you do not lose what you have worked for, but that you may be rewarded fully (2 John 8).

See, the Lord is coming with thousands upon thousands of his holy ones to judge everyone, and to convict all the ungodly of all the ungodly acts they have done in the ungodly way, and of all the harsh words ungodly sinners have spoken against him (Jude 14, 15).

Look, he is coming with the clouds, and every eye will see him, even those who pierced him; and all the peoples of the earth will mourn because of him. So shall it be! Amen (Revelation 1:7).

John ends the New Testament with the words, "He who testifies to these things says, 'Yes, I am coming soon!' Amen. Come, Lord Jesus. The grace of the Lord Jesus be with God's people. Amen."

Don't let your Timex fool you. He is coming back. When? We will discuss that next.

2

When
Is He Coming Back?

"What did he say?" That was my first question when Julia came out of the doctor's office. Julia was two weeks overdue with our third child. Needless to say, we were getting anxious.

"He said the baby is not coming soon, and he will see me next week," she told me.

That was not good news for us, but we decided to eat out at a restaurant before returning home. A half hour later we were sitting at a table waiting for the waitress to bring our order when I noticed a strange look on Julia's face. "What's wrong?" I queried.

"Oh, nothing—at least I don't think so."

We had eaten four or five bites of our supper when she announced that she was having labor pains. I did the only thing fathers seem to be able to do at such a time. I checked the second hand on my watch and started keeping track of the pains and the timing. Soon the pains were four minutes apart. We left the food on the table and headed for the hospital. Julia was immediately put in the labor room, and not long afterward, Rhonda was born.

But what about the words from the expert who said the baby was not coming soon? In having four children, I have discovered that when it comes to pinpointing the birth of a child, there is no such person as an expert.

We Want a Clue

We have some of the same anxieties about the second coming of Jesus that we have about the coming of a new baby. We would like to know exactly when it will happen. But after spending a few years studying the Bible, reading the predictions from the "experts," and discussing the topic with people, I have discovered that there is no such person as an expert when it comes to pinpointing *when* Jesus will come back.

It is not a new fad to try to discover exactly when Jesus will return. More than once the apostles of Jesus tried to get Him to give them a clue about the time. During the last week prior to Jesus' crucifixion, His apostles asked the question that must have been burning within them: "Tell us . . . when will this happen, and what will be the sign of your coming and of the end of the age?" (Matthew 24:3). After His resurrection and just before the ascension, they asked, "Lord, are you at this time going to restore the kingdom to Israel?" (Acts 1:6). Don't get upset with people who want to know when Jesus is coming back. At least they do believe He *is* coming back. In that they are right.

As it isn't new to try to discover when He is returning, neither is it a new gimmick to try to "invent" the time He will return and then announce it to everyone. Anyone who tells exactly when Jesus will return is saying he has an "inside track" on God's plans. He can demand attention. He can set himself up as someone for the multitudes to follow. He can keep people so hooked on him as a person and as an "expert" that they will believe and do whatever he tells them. Many times in history such people have been successful in leading others to sell their possessions and move to another location to wait for the date that was announced for Jesus' return.

Even in Paul's day some Christians were eager to know the date of the second coming. That is why Paul wrote, "Now, brothers, about times and dates we do not need to write to you" (1 Thessalonians 5:1). Why not? Paul immediately explained, "For you know very well that the day of the Lord will come like a thief in the night" (5:2). Somehow we slide right over this teaching of Paul and rush out to buy the book that has the latest theory about the exact date of Jesus' return. But we should not get too upset over this tendency; even the Thessalonians did not let Paul's teaching sink in.

Between Paul's first letter to them and his second, some of the Christians in Thessalonica had been duped into thinking that Jesus had already returned, and they had missed it. Thus Paul wrote to them again about this issue: "Now we request you, brethren, with regard to the coming of our Lord Jesus Christ, and our gathering together to Him, that you may not be quickly shaken from your composure or be disturbed either by a spirit or a message or a letter as if from us, to the effect that the day of the Lord has come" (2 Thessalonians 2:1, 2, NAS.) The New International Version reads "some prophecy," instead of "spirit," but the literal translation is "spirit."

Could anyone possibly think that Jesus had already returned? Yes, and many still do today. Some teach that Jesus returned in A.D. 70 at the destruction of Jerusalem. Proponents of that position have put together Scripture verses that "prove" their point and have deceived many Christians.

How could the Thessalonians have been so deceived? The same way Christians today can. Paul mentioned three things that were and still are powerful psychological pulls that attract people to deception: (a) a spirit, (b) a message, (c) a "letter as if from us." A person who convinces others that he has a special dispensation of the

17

Holy Spirit can claim to have received a message from the Spirit. That is exciting and arouses our curiosity. Who wouldn't want to listen to someone who claims to have had a special experience with the Spirit and now can tell us about the second coming?

The third approach may not be as sensational, but it attracts people with its logic. Someone uses the words of the apostles to prove the point. He pulls verses out of context, strings them together in another way, and announces, "This is what the apostle said." Another way this approach is used is a bit more exciting—someone claims that *he* is an apostle, so whatever he says or writes is apostolic and true.

There are also those who write that current events are specifically prophesied in the Bible and are proof that the end has come or is near. Such teachings have been used in every century of Christianity. It is easy to find a text that someone thinks fits any current event. But there are no texts that *clearly* discuss events such as the oil crisis, the rise of the Russians, the use of computers, and other recent happenings. Such things are "read into" the texts. Humans are inventive and creative creatures and can read almost anything into some Scripture text.

No One Knows

Where does that leave us then in regard to the time of Jesus' return? I want to be as charitable as I can at this point, but I also want to be very clear. *Do not fall for anyone who claims to have "inside information" about when Jesus will return.* He is like the doctor who told us the baby would not come soon. Neither he nor we knew *when* that baby's arrival would be. It is the same with the teachings of Jesus and the apostles concerning the times, dates, or seasons of the second coming. No one but God knows.

When the apostles asked Jesus about the timing of His kingdom, Jesus told them what should be accepted by all of us: "It is not for you to know the times or dates the Father has set by His own authority" (Acts 1:7). Jesus himself did not know when His return would be. No disciple of His knew; for Jesus said, "A student is not above his teacher, but everyone who is fully trained will be like his teacher" (Luke 6:40).

When we have been "fully trained" on the issue of the second coming, we will admit that we do not know when Jesus will return. This should not be a threat to our egos; Jesus' ego was not threatened by it—and He was God's equal partner! Jesus' lack of knowledge in this area did not diminish His influence with His students either. If we think we know what Jesus did not know, we are among the blind trying to lead the blind. Jesus was warning against this (Luke 6:39, 40).

How do we know Jesus did not have this knowledge? He said He didn't: "No one knows about that day or hour, not even the angels in heaven, nor the Son, but only the Father" (Matthew 24:36). On that occasion, Jesus was giving His apostles four warnings:

1. Don't connect the second coming with other earthly events as if the two have to coincide. The apostles had thought that the return of Jesus and the destruction of the temple would coincide (Matthew 24:1-3), but they were wrong.

2. Don't believe reports about the second coming. Many will claim to be the returned Messiah—ignore them (Matthew 24:4, 5). "So if anyone tells you, 'There he is, out in the desert,' do not go out; or 'Here he is, in the inner rooms,' do not believe it" (Matthew 24:26).

3. Don't allow catastrophies or tragedies to make you think the second coming has to follow immediately.

You will hear of wars and rumors of wars, but see to it that you are not alarmed. Such things must happen, *but the end is still to come*. Nation will rise against nation, and kingdom against kingdom.

There will be famines and earthquakes in various places. All these are the *beginning* of birth pains (Matthew 24:6-8, italics mine. See also Mark 13 and Luke 21).

The beginning of birth pains does not tell us exactly *when* the baby will come; it only tells us *that* he is coming. Jesus will return!

4. False prophets will arise with their "great signs" (Matthew 24:23-25). Even now some people continuously point out "great signs" of the end time. But Jesus said when we see the heavenly bodies shaken and see the "Son of Man coming in a cloud with power and great glory," we should stand up and lift up our heads because our redemption is near (Luke 21:26-28). The point is this: When we *see* Him coming, that is the time!

Those who read every verse in Matthew 24 and then come up with a detailed schedule of dates seem to overlook the fact that after Jesus made all these statements He said, "No one knows." He must have known that people would try to take His words and figure out the exact date, for He stressed six different times that no one knows:

1. "No one knows about that day or hour, not even the angels in heaven, nor the Son, but only the Father" (Matthew 24:36). Not even the heavenly beings know.

2. Jesus compared the ignorance about the time of the second coming with the ignorance about the time of the flood in Noah's day. The people in that day did not know "until the flood came and took them all away. That is how it will be at the coming of the Son of Man" (Matthew 24:37-39). Just as they did not know until the flood was upon them, we will not know until Jesus comes.

3. You do not know on what day your Lord will come" (Matthew 24:42). Jesus was speaking to His apostles; thus we are assured that the apostles did not know.

4. Jesus compared the ignorance about the time of the second coming with the ignorance about when a thief

would strike. If a property owner knew when a thief would come, he would be ready and waiting for him. "So you also must be ready, because the Son of Man will come at an hour when you do not expect him" (Matthew 24:44).

5. Jesus warned against thinking that the time of His return is so far off that we can ignore it (Matthew 24:45-51). We cannot figure out the date ahead of time, but we dare not suppose it is far in the future. "The master of that servant will come on a day when he does not expect him and at an hour he is not aware of" (24:50).

6. Jesus warned against thinking that we have plenty of time to get our lives in order. He illustrated such a fallacy with the parable of the ten virgins. Five virgins were not prepared, and when the bridegroom came it was too late to prepare (Matthew 25:1-12). When Jesus appears there will be no time to get ready. "Therefore keep watch, because you do not know the day or the hour" (25:13).

Some people tell us Christ will not come for a long time because first there must be some "signs" that have not yet happened. We should not be deceived by such talk. It is a mistake to suppose that Jesus must come very soon (2 Thessalonians 2:3), but it is also a mistake to suppose that He cannot come this very day (1 Thessalonians 4:15-17). Paul was not wrong to think Jesus could return any day—even before the Iranian crisis, the rise of Communism, or the rebuilding of the temple.

Be Ready

We must conclude that the second coming of Jesus will be a surprise because no one can figure out the hour or date or season. Jesus will come as a thief—no telltale signs ahead of time, no pre-announcement. "You do not know the day or the hour (Matthew 25:13).

And that day will close on you unexpectedly like a trap (Luke 21:34).

> You know very well that the day of the Lord will come like a thief in the night (1 Thessalonians 5:2).

> But the day of the Lord will come like a thief (2 Peter 3:10).

> I will come like a thief, and you will not know at what time I will come to you (Revelation 3:3).

> Behold, I come like a thief! Blessed is he who stays awake and keeps his clothes with him, so that he may not go naked and be shamefully exposed (Revelation 16:15).

From Luke through Revelation, Jesus did not change His plan to return as a thief. I doubt very much that He has given any modern-day "prophet" a special revelation about the time of His return.

Jesus promised that the Holy Spirit would guide His apostles into *all* truth (John 16:13). After the resurrection, Jesus opened the minds of the apostles to understand the Scriptures (Luke 24:45), but none of them revealed to us when Jesus would return. Why not? They did not know. We have one major practical teaching about it—Be ready! (Matthew 24:42, 44, 45; 25:13; 1 Thessalonians 5:6; 2 Peter 3:11; Revelation 3:3; 16:15).

One afternoon while John Wesley was hoeing his garden a friend asked him, "John, what would you do if you knew for certain that Jesus would return this afternoon?"

"I'd go right on hoeing my garden," John Wesley replied.

By that reply, he was saying that his life was in order. The question is this: Are you ready? Am I? Would we be doing anything differently if we knew for certain that Jesus would return today? There are two things you can know for certain: He is coming back, and it will be a surprise.

3

How
Is He Coming Back?

During the post-depression days when we had no money to buy board games for the family to play, we invented our own games. One that was quite popular everywhere was called "Button, button, who's got the button?" A button was passed from hand to hand and from person to person, and the one who was "it" had to guess who had the button at a set time. We are playing a similar guessing game today about the date of the return of Jesus. We could call it "The date, the date, who's got the exact date?" But as we have learned thus far, no one knows the exact date of Jesus' return except for the Heavenly Father, who will bring it about "in his own time" (1 Timothy 6:15).

Although we cannot know in advance when Jesus will return, we can know some of the things that will accompany His return. Yet even at this point there are wide differences in the opinions held by sincere Christians. Some of these different views are referred to as millennial theories. *Millennium* literally means "thousand years." Specifically it is used of the thousand years mentioned in

Revelation 20:1-6. Millennial theories concern those years and sometimes include other events connected with the second coming of Christ.

The Millennial Theories

The three basic millennial theories are called post-millennial, pre-millennial, and a-millennial. Each of these views is held by Christians. It would be a serious mistake to evaluate a person's sincerity or his salvation by his millennial position. On the Day of Judgment, God will not give us a final exam about the millennium to determine our eternal destination. There will be people in Heaven who hold all three of these theories about the second coming.

No doubt there will also be a host of people in Heaven who have never heard about any millennial theory. They would not be able to pronounce the word, let alone spell it. They will not have spent any time figuring out the events of the second coming. Instead, they will have lived their lives with simple faith in Jesus as the Son of God. Yes, they will be there with all those who thought they had the millennial problem all figured out.

If we, with all our different views, can live together in peace in Heaven, we should practice living in peace on the earth now. Whom God has united in Jesus, may the millennial opinions not divide!

These three theories hold certain beliefs in common: (1) belief that the Bible is the inspired word of God, (2) belief that Jesus is divine, (3) belief that Jesus died for our sins, (4) belief that Jesus is coming back, (5) belief that those outside of Christ will go to Hell, while those in Christ will go to Heaven.

These theories differ at several points, such as the nature of the church, the nature of the reign of Christ, the binding of Satan, the salvation of Israel, the antichrist, and the accomplishments that will take place at the second coming.

24

The post-millennialist believes that Jesus Christ will not return until the end of a long period of time (a millennium) during which life on earth will be characterized by a "golden age" of peace because of the influence of the church.

The pre-millennialist believes that there will be a general falling apart of life on earth. Life will not get better but worse. There will be a time of great tribulation; then Christ will come. Christ will then set up an earthly reign for one thousand years. Only after these years pass will the end of the world come with "a new heaven and a new earth."

The a-millennialist believes that we are now living in the last days (the millennium) and that Jesus may return at any second. He believes that Jesus has not returned yet because God wants to give sinners more time to repent—not because the golden age or the tribulation has not yet come.

The proponents of each theory (at least some who major in studying about the end-time events) think they have figured out all the sequences and events that will lead to (or "force") Jesus' return. But I suspect that Jesus' will return when God says so in spite of our systematic theology. No one should be so set in having the end-time figured out that he will be disappointed at Christ's return because it is not when or how he has decided it will be.

Fights and fusses about the millennial issue have gotten so far out of hand among some Christians that they have forgotten who their spiritual enemy is. Our enemy is not another Christian who has a different view about the second coming. Our enemy is Satan, who loves to have us bicker about things that we cannot possibly alter. It must grieve our Heavenly Father to watch how some of us treat His children in "games that Christians play." Too many egos are trying to defend their pet opinions rather than defend Emmanuel. When the prevailing attitude is

"I've got to prove I'm right," fellowship within the family of God is hurt.

We should be spending our time and energy mastering life on earth so that when Christ does return, regardless of when He comes or what events accompany His coming, we will be ready. Let us check our waiting, not our theories about the end of time.

Regardless of the theories men hold, the Bible is clear about certain events connected with Christ's return. We do not need to be deceived about them.

The Sounds

Although Jesus will come unexpectedly as a thief in the night, He will not step in and out silently as a thief does. No, He will return in noisy excitement and with a loud fanfare. "For the Lord himself will come down from heaven, with a loud command, with the voice of the archangel and with the trumpet call of God" (1 Thessalonians 4:16; 1 Corinthians 15:51, 52).

The trumpets will blast, and the command will be loud. The trumpets and the command will serve the same purpose. Trumpets were used to assemble God's people, and the command will be to gather together. Even the dead will hear the blast and the command to assemble: "The dead in Christ will rise" (1 Corinthians 15:51, 52; 1 Thessalonians 4:16). Yes, Jesus' return will be heard.

The Sights

When Jesus ascended into Heaven, the apostles stared into the sky. For a few moments they seemed to be paralyzed by His departure. But such paralysis does little for the kingdom of God. So two men dressed in white broke the spell by saying, "Men of Galilee . . . why do you stand here looking into the sky? This same Jesus, who has been taken from you into heaven, will come back in the same way you have seen him go into heaven" (Acts 1:11). What is that "same way"? He was "taken up be-

26

fore their very eyes" (Acts 1:9); He will come down before our very eyes. He was taken up in a cloud (Acts 1:9); He will return in a cloud.

Jesus declared, "But I say to all of you: In the future you will see the Son of Man . . . coming on the clouds of heaven" (Matthew 26:64). Two points are made: He will be seen, and He will come on the clouds. John also made these points clear: "Look, he is coming with the clouds, and every eye will see him, even those who pierced him" (Revelation 1:7). Some people get concerned about John's statement: they wonder how every person on both sides of the globe can see Jesus. How is it possible? I do not know. Neither do I know how God could split the Red Sea, or how Jesus could walk on water, or how Jesus could ascend in a cloud. But I do know that as the heavens are higher than the earth, so are God's ways higher than ours (Isaiah 55:9). God can do it—and He will not need closed-circuit television. It is not for us to know *how* God will do it, but it is for us to believe that He *will* do it.

The Saints

We will see Jesus, but He will not be alone. He will come with angels (Matthew 25:31), with "thousands upon thousands of His holy ones" (Jude 14). God will also "bring with Jesus those who have fallen asleep in him" (1 Thessalonians 4:14; see also Colossians 3:4). As Jesus returns, the dead in Christ will arise from wherever they are and join Him (1 Thessalonians 4:16).

Where are the dead in Christ now? While some believe they are in some kind of sleeping state in their graves, the New Testament suggests something much grander than that. Paul said that "to live is Christ and to die is gain" (Philippians 1:21). How could it be gain if physical death separated us from Christ in some kind of "sleep"? It is gain to die in Christ, because at death we are ushered into His presence. That is what Paul meant when he said that to be away from the body is to be at home with the Lord (2 Corinthians 5:6-8).

Jesus told a parable that shows us that a godly person who died was very consciously in "Abraham's bosom" (Luke 16:19-31). On the mount of transfiguration, two people appeared with Jesus. One of them had died centuries earlier, and the other had been taken to Heaven without dying (Matthew 17:1-3; Deuteronomy 34:5; 2 Kings 2:11). They could appear because they continued to live in the presence of God. Jesus criticized the Sadducees for not believing in a resurrection, citing the fact that God is the God of Abraham, Isaac, and Jacob. He pointed out that God is not a God of the dead but of the living (Matthew 22:29-32). Abraham, Isaac, and Jacob are alive, not dead.

While we do not know the details of what happens right after a person dies physically, we do know that Jesus promised that anyone who hears His word and believes in God "has crossed over from death to life" (John 5:24) and "whoever lives and believes in me will never die" (John 11:26).

When Jesus brings the saints who have died with Him, a grand reunion will take place. "After that, we who are still alive and are left will be caught up with them in the clouds to meet the Lord in the air. And so we will be with the Lord forever" (1 Thessalonians 4:17).

John also wrote about this reunion in Revelation 21:1-14:

> Then I saw a new heaven and a new earth, for the first heaven and the first earth had passed away, and there was no longer any sea. I saw the Holy City, the new Jerusalem, coming down out of heaven from God, prepared as a bride beautifully dressed for her husband. And I heard a loud voice from the throne saying, "Now the dwelling of God is with men, and he will live with them. They will be

his people, and God himself will be with them and be their God. He will wipe every tear from their eyes. There will be no more death or mourning or crying or pain, for the old order of things has passed away."

The Cosmic Events

Not only will the return of Jesus be experienced by our seeing, our hearing, and our gathering together, but also by the catastrophic changes that will occur in nature: "The sun will be darkened, and the moon will not give its light; the stars will fall from the sky, and the heavenly bodies will be shaken" (Matthew 24:29).

Right now nature is being held together by Christ (Colossians 1:17); but when He returns, He will let go. Nature as we know it will fall apart: "The heavens will disappear with a roar; the elements will be destroyed by fire, and the earth and everything in it will be laid bare" (2 Peter 3:10).

This cosmic change will be the sign that Jesus is returning, but it will allow no time for us to get ready. He will be here!

At that time the sign of the Son of Man will appear in the sky, and all the nations of the earth will mourn. They will see the Son of Man coming on the clouds of the sky, with power and great glory. And he will send his angels with a loud trumpet call, and they will gather his elect from the four winds, from one end of the heavens to the other (Matthew 24:30, 31).

When the sun, moon, and stars change, we will see Jesus and His angels, and we will hear the blast. Jesus will be accompanied by the saints, and the grand reunion of the saved on earth with the saved in Heaven will take place.

Conclusion

While we may still be prone to want to know "when" and more details about the "how," Peter leads us to think properly:

> Since everything will be destroyed in this way, what kind of people ought you to be? You ought to live holy and godly lives as you look forward to the day of God. . . . So then, dear friends, since you are looking forward to this, make every effort to be found spotless, blameless and at peace with him (2 Peter 3:11-14).

Since we know for a surety that Jesus will return, we must be most concerned about how we are living in the now. Next we will consider *why* Jesus is returning to earth.

4

Why

Is He Coming Back?

—To Reveal That He Is Lord

Return to planet earth? Why would Jesus want to return after the way people of earth treated Him? Yet Jesus left with the promise, "I shall return."

Although we can keep guessing about when He will return—and miss every guess—we do not have to guess about *why* He will return. Out of the graciousness of God, He has revealed the reasons to us for our well-being. He tells us both good news and bad news. His return will be good news for those who have loved, trusted, and followed Him. But His return will be bad news for those who have shunned Him. It will be earth's final day, and the Lord's finest hour.

The day of Jesus' return is referred to in many different ways in the New Testament:

the day the Son of Man is revealed (Luke 17:30)
the last day (John 6:40, 44, 54)
the great and glorious day of the Lord (Acts 2:20)
the day of God's wrath (Romans 2:5)
the day of the Lord (1 Corinthians 5:5)

the day of the Lord Jesus (2 Corinthians 1:14)
the day of redemption (Ephesians 4:30)
the day of Christ Jesus (Philippians 1:6)
the day of Christ (Philippians 1:10; 2:16)
the day of God (2 Peter 3:12)
the great day (Jude 6)
the great day of their wrath (Revelation 6:17)

The second coming of Jesus was so important to the early Christians that they could refer to it as simply "the day" (1 Corinthians 3:13; Hebrews 10:25) and "that day" (2 Timothy 1:12, 18; 4:8).

A Day of Acknowledging Him

One of the reasons God has set a time for Jesus to return to earth is to insure that His Son receives the honor on earth that He deserves. God will not allow the people who reject Jesus to have the last word. Their denial of Jesus will not be their last evaluation of Him. God "exalted him to the highest place and gave him the name that is above every name" (Philippians 2:9). And God will see to it that everyone acknowledges the truth about Jesus. The day Jesus returns will be the day Jesus is revealed (Luke 17:30) so clearly "that at the name of Jesus every knee should bow, in heaven and on earth and under the earth, and every tongue confess that Jesus Christ is Lord, to the glory of God the Father" (Philippians 2:10, 11).

As Jesus starts to return, those who rejected Him will instantly know how wrong they were. They will not want to admit their error. In fact, they will hide "in caves and among the rocks of the mountains" and will call "to the mountains and the rocks, 'Fall on us and hide us from the face of him who sits on the throne and from the wrath of the Lamb' " (Revelation 6:15, 16). But they will have to face up to the reality of who Jesus was, is, and always will be—The Lord.

How tragic that some will confess Him on that day to their own condemnation! Jesus said the universal confession on that day will not result in salvation for those who have not confessed Him before that day: "If anyone is ashamed of me and my words in this adulterous and sinful generation, the Son of Man will be ashamed of him when he comes in his Father's glory with the holy angels" (Mark 8:38). Confessing Jesus prior to the second coming does not mean simply repeating Peter's confession, "You are the Christ, the Son of the Living God" (Matthew 16:16). Confession also involves adopting Christ's lifestyle in the midst of an adulterous and sinful environment. It means giving Him first place, not putting Him and His teachings on the back burner because what He says and how He lived do not jive with the modern trends.

We must not put off thoughts of the "day of the Lord" until we see Jesus coming in the clouds. That final day is coming nearer, ever nearer. With that in mind the writer of Hebrews said, "Let us not give up meeting together, as some are in the habit of doing, but let us encourage one another—and all the more as you see the Day approaching" (Hebrews 10:25). We must meet together *now* to affirm His lordship, or our meeting together *then* will condemn us.

It is not enough to set aside one day of the week as "the Lord's Day" and ignore His lordship over all the other days. Jesus is Lord of every day. So to await the day of the Lord is to acknowledge Him every day exactly as we shall acknowledge Him on that special day.

A Day of Serving Him

One thing we will do on the day of the Lord (that final day) will be to offer ourselves in service to Him forever. We read that God's people will be serving Him night and day in Heaven (Revelation 7:15). But we cannot be His servants then if we will not be His servants now.

Jesus was making that point clear in several of the parables He told shortly before He went to the cross. One of those parables dealt with a father and two sons. One son said he would not work in the vineyard, but later he did. The other son promised to work, but did not do it. His "service" was lip service only. Jesus said the first son did what the father wanted (Matthew 21:28-32). It is easy to be religious on Sunday morning and not actually work in the vineyard on Monday. Let's live every day with Heaven in mind. If we are to serve Him there and then, we must serve Him here and now (Matthew 21:31).

Jesus immediately followed that parable with a similar one. A landowner eventually destroyed those people who did work in his vineyard but rejected the lordship of his son over their labors (Matthew 21:33-46). What a lesson for those of us who are pragmatic workaholics! Sometimes it is easy to think that God will *have* to save us because we have done so much for Him. But in the process of staying busy, we have done our own work in our own way. We have actually worked for ourselves and forgotten the lordship of Jesus over our lives.

Jesus told still another parable about a person who accepted the invitation to a wedding banquet without accepting the corresponding responsibilities (Matthew 22:1-14). The point of all of these parables is that service must be service in actuality, not pretense. When I was a boy growing up, one of my favorite Saturday morning radio programs was "Let's Pretend." I loved to pretend. That program was okay for children, but it should not be the pattern for the Christian life. We must not take God's grace and only pretend we are doing something with it.

Jesus also told the parables of the ten virgins and the talents amidst a discussion of how to be ready for the second coming. In the latter part of Matthew 24, He gave plain and forceful warnings to be ready. Then He told these two parables in Matthew 25, followed by still more discussion of the second coming.

Both of these parables teach the same thing from different angles: *serve now*. Five of the virgins did nothing except look for the coming of the bridegroom. They were moral (virgins); they were regular attenders (meeting with the others). But they were not ready when the bridegroom came. In the parable of the talents, one servant had received a gift from the master, but did no service with it. He hid it so he would be secure when the master returned. But his "nothingness" drew from his master the label "worthless servant," and he was condemned.

Offering our service to Jesus does not mean that we drop out of society and do nothing but sing songs, pray, and take Communion. It means, "Whatever you do, work at it with all your heart, as working for the Lord, not for men" (Colossians 3:23). Paul was saying that what we do in our secular jobs should be done for the Lord. For our culture, he is talking about how we do our work on the assembly line, behind the wheel of a truck, in the office, in the field, in the classroom, etc. Lest you think I am taking this verse out of context to refer to the second coming, note the rest of the sentence: "Since you know that you will receive an inheritance from the Lord as a reward" (Colossians 3:24). Why does Paul connect our spiritual reward to our secular work? Because *every* day is to be the Lord's. Consequently, we are to be serving the Lord Jesus on our jobs every day.

For the Christian, no job is merely "secular." Every job is holy when we do it "with sincerity of heart and reverence for the Lord" (Colossians 3:22). Our jobs take on more "service significance" when we do them as if Jesus Christ were the user of our product, as if Jesus Christ were our foreman, as if Jesus Christ were the owner of the company, as if Jesus Christ were the one who writes our paychecks.

And in a real sense, Jesus is all of these. He does use our products as He lives in the people who use them. Whatever we do for or against Christians we do for or against Jesus. If we try to cheat people by doing shoddy work or using defective materials, we are cheating Jesus.

Jesus Christ is our foreman, our Master. Paul wrote these instructions:

> Slaves, obey your earthly masters with respect and fear, and with sincerity of heart, just as you would obey Christ. Obey them not only to win their favor when their eye is on you, but like slaves of Christ, doing the will of God from your heart. Serve wholeheartedly, as if you were serving the Lord, not men (Ephesians 6:5-7).

Jesus is also the co-owner (with His Father) of the company. Many stockholders and boards of directors do not know that yet, but they will someday. We must do the kind of work we should, and do it without complaint about the pay, just as if Jesus were sitting in the front office.

What does Jesus' lordship mean at a practical level on our jobs? It means we will not call in sick when we are not. We will not use second-rate materials and charge for first-class ones. We will not claim to have replaced parts or done repair work when we haven't. We will not take more than the allowed time for lunch and coffee breaks. We will not use the WATS line for personal phone calls. We will not use company time to write personal letters. We will not try to undermine our fellow workers or our superiors. We will do for the company what we would like the workers to do for us if we owned the company. We will not drop out of the work force to wait for Jesus to return. Paul spoke harshly against idleness (2 Thessalonians 3:6-13) with this admoniton: "If a man will not work, he shall not eat."

Yes, we are to await the coming of the "day of the Lord" by treating every day as His day. We are to be His servants in every experience of life—not only on the job.

When we live with our families as He would have us live, then He is the Lord of that day. When we handle our lesiure time as He would, then He is the Lord of that day. When we live as His laborers on the job, then He is the Lord of that day. When we use our lives to benefit others, then He is the Lord of that day. When we meet together with God's people in worship, then He is the Lord of that day.

A Day of Singing

That final day will not only begin an eternity of our acknowledging and serving Him, but will also begin an eternity of our singing a "new song" of victory and praise to Him (Revelation 5:9, 10; 14:3; 15:3, 4). On that day we will sing those kinds of songs that will echo throughout Heaven and eternity, praising Jesus and acknowledging that He is Lord. Note some example of the heavenly music that is to be:

Holy, holy, holy is the Lord God Almighty, who was, and is, and is to come (Revelation 4:8).

You are worthy, our Lord and God, to receive glory and honor and power, for you created all things, and by your will they were created and have their being (Revelation 4:11).

You are worthy to take the scroll and to open its seals, because you were slain, and with your blood you purchased men for God from every tribe and language and people and nation. You have made them to be a kingdom and priests to serve our God, and they will reign on the earth (Revelation 5:9, 10).

Worthy is the Lamb, who was slain, to receive power and wealth and wisdom and strength and honor and glory and praise! (Revelation 5:12).

To him who sits on the throne and to the Lamb be praise and honor and glory and power for ever and ever! (Revelation 5:13).

Salvation belongs to our God, who sits on the throne, and to the Lamb (Revelation 7:10).

Amen! Praise and glory and wisdom and thanks and honor and power and strength be to our God forever and ever. Amen! (Revelation 7:12).

Great and marvelous are our deeds, Lord God Almighty. Just and true are your ways, King of the ages (Revelation 15:3).

But if we want to be singing to His glory then, we must be singing to His glory now. "Let the word of Christ dwell in you richly as you teach and admonish one another with all wisdom, and as you sing psalms, hymns and spiritual songs with gratitude in your hearts to God" (Colossians 3:16, see also Ephesians 5:19).

Conclusion

Any day is Jesus' day if we bow our knees in humble submission to Him, use our lips to confess His lordship, offer our lives in His service, and open our hearts to sing praises to His name. May the day He returns not be the first "day of the Lord" that we experience. If it is, it will be too late. Instead may that day merely be the day that puts a crown on every other day that we have lived as His.

He is Lord! *That* day will prove it to everyone. In the meantime, may we practice having Him as Lord of our lives before the eyes of everyone.

Why

Is He Coming Back?

—To Judge

When Jesus comes back, He will not come with His eyes closed to what has been happening on earth. His return will be a day of reckoning for us all. He declared, "Behold, I am coming soon! My reward is with me, and I will give to everyone according to what he has done" (Revelation 22:12).

Man did not have the first word in history, and he will not have the last word. Our Lord will. For that reason He is called "the Alpha and the Omega, the First and the Last, the Beginning and the End" (Revelation 22:13). Alpha and Omega are the first and last letters in the Greek alphabet: the statement above is similar to saying, "Jesus is the A and Z of history." When Jesus finishes what He will say on that day, there will not be a single letter anyone can add to it. No one will be able to veto or alter what Jesus says. He will come not only as Lord, but also as Judge—the supreme Judge. It is no wonder that the day of His coming is also called the Day of Judgment. Let's look at some of the Scriptures where we see that name or the idea it expresses.

I tell you the truth, it will be more bearable for Sodom and Gomorrah on the *day of judgment* than for that town (Matthew 10:15, see also 11:22-24).

But I tell you that men will have to give account on the *day of judgment* for every careless word they have spoken (Matthew 12:36).

For he has set a *day* when he will *judge* the world with justice by the man he has appointed (Acts 17:31).

This will take place on the *day* when God will *judge* men's secrets through Jesus Christ, as my gospel declares (Romans 2:16).

If this is so, then the Lord knows how to rescue godly men from trials and to hold the unrighteous for the *day of judgment* (2 Peter 2:9).

By the same word the present heavens and earth are reserved for fire, being kept for the *day of judgment* and destruction of ungodly men (2 Peter 3:7).

Love is made complete among us so that we will have confidence on the *day of judgment,* because in this world we are like him (1 John 4:17).

And the angels who did not keep their positions of authority but abandoned their own home—these he has kept in darkness, bound with everlasting chains for *judgment on the great Day* (Jude 6).

In addition to calling that great day the "day of judgment," the Bible is saturated with teachings about man's judgment. Following is just a sampling:

For we will all stand before God's judgment seat (Romans 14:10).

Just as man is destined to die once, and after that to face judgment (Hebrews 9:27).

For we know him who said, "It is mine to avenge; I will repay," and again, "The Lord will judge his people" (Hebrews 10:30).

But they will have to give account to him who is ready to judge the living and the dead (1 Peter 4:5).

See, the Lord is coming with thousands upon thousands of his holy ones to judge everyone (Jude 14, 15).

And I saw the dead, great and small, standing before the throne, and books were opened. Another book was opened, which is the book of life. The dead were judged according to what they had done as recorded in the books (Revelation 20:12).

The Christian and Judgment

I used to think about the Day of Judgment as a dreadful happening full of bad news. I can remember thinking that on that day God would have me stand before everyone who has ever known me personally or known about me and would "spill the beans" by letting everyone know all the mistakes I had made.

But God has promised to forget about our sins as He forgives them: "For I will forgive their wickedness and will remember their sins no more" (Hebrews 8:12. See also Hebrews 10:17). We are promised that our sins are washed away (Acts 22:16) and wiped out (Acts 3:19). The words *wiped out* were used to describe the melting of letters on a wax tablet so they could never again be seen.

41

That is what God does when He forgives sin. He will not remember our sins on the Day of Judgment. Some may ask, "But how can God forget anything?" God can forget anything that He remembers to forget. He will not "tattle" on us on the Day of Judgment.

I can also remember thinking that at Jesus' return I should run to the hills and cry for the rocks to fall on me. How foolish I was! The Christian has no need to fear the Day of Judgment. It is true that "the wages of sin is death," but it is equally true that "the gift of God is eternal life in Christ Jesus our Lord" (Romans 6:23). The person who is in Christ is in salvation. "Therefore, there is now no condemnation for those who are in Christ Jesus" (Romans 8:1).

I also used to believe that no one could know whether or not he was saved until that final day when he would watch to see how his bad deeds stacked up against his good deeds. Whichever stack was the taller would determine one's eternity. That belief was also foolish, for we are not saved or condemned by such scorekeeping. We are saved or condemned by whether we are in Christ or outside of Christ. That is the good news.

For it is by grace you have been saved, through faith—and this is not from yourselves, it is the gift of God (Ephesians 2:8).

For God so loved the world that he gave his one and only Son, that whoever believes in him shall not perish but have eternal life. . . . Whoever believes in him is not condemned, but whoever does not believe stands condemned already because he has not believed in the name of God's one and only Son (John 3:16-18).

And this is the testimony: God has given us eternal life, and this life is in His Son. He who has the Son

42

has life: he who does not have the Son of God does not have life (1 John 5:11, 12).

When Jesus returns, the Christian is not to run away from Him as if terrified. Instead the Christian will run with praise toward Him. "And now, dear children, continue in him, so that when he appears we may be confident and unashamed before him at his coming" (1 John 2:28). The Christian can have confidence, not cowardice, on the Day of Judgment because he relies on the love of God and manifests that love in his own life.

And so we know and rely on the love God has for us. God is love. Whoever lives in love lives in God, and God in him. Love is made complete among us so that we will have confidence on the day of judgment, because in this world we are like him (1 John 4:16, 17).

Yes, there is salvation in Jesus. But notice the two qualifications: "continue in Him" and "whoever lives in love lives in God" (1 John 2:28; 4:16). It is not enough to simply go through some religious rituals and claim, "I am in Christ, so I have the Day of Judgment all taken care of." The person who is truly in Christ must demonstrate it by living as Christ lives. "Whoever claims to live in him must walk as Jesus did" (1 John 2:6). That does not mean that we will never sin again. We will (1 John 1:8; 2:1). But it does mean that the Christian way is dominant in our lives.

The dominant mark of the Christian who is walking in Jesus is love. Jesus declared, "All men will know that you are my disciples if you love one another" (John 13:35). And that love is to be as Christ loved. "As I have loved you, so you must love one another" (John 13:34). "My command is this: Love each other as I have loved you" (John 15:12).

If we are living and loving as we should, the Day of Judgment will be good news for us. But what can we do specifically to demonstrate right now the type of love that will assure us on the Day of Judgment? One way is forgiveness.

Forgiveness

If God has forgiven us, we *must* forgive others.

> For if you forgive men when they sin against you, your heavenly Father will also forgive you. But if you do not forgive men their sins, your Father will not forgive your sins (Matthew 6:14, 15).

When one knows what it means to need forgiveness and receive it, he becomes a broken person who is humbled enough to forgive others. Until our hearts are broken down by sin and until we find ourselves crying out to God for forgiveness, we hang on too much to our own egos. We inwardly believe that God saves us because we really deserve it. We think we are pretty good folks and do a lot for God, so we deserve salvation. When we think like that, we find it hard to forgive others when they fall. We think we are better than they are; after all, they should have known better than to make those mistakes.

When we truly sense the need for forgiveness, when we truly sense our own faults and weaknesses, then we realize that we are on the level of everyone else— that we are simply beggars, made poor by sin, in need of God's forgiveness and salvation. It is then that we can extend forgiveness to others and mean it.

God will judge us by the same standard we use to judge others. Jesus said, "For in the same way you judge others, you will be judged, and with the measure you use, it will be measured to you" (Matthew 7:2). James declared, "Judgment without mercy will be shown to anyone who has not been merciful. Mercy triumphs over judgment" (James 2:13). Do we exercise grace or retaliation? Mercy or harshness? Forgetfulness or remembering? Reconciliation or animosity?

A major tragedy in the church is when one member will not forgive another. It may be true that the initial sin caused disharmony and hurt, but the unforgiving reaction may be a bigger sin in that it perpetuates the disharmony and hurt. The ministry of reconciliation should be demonstrated best within the church. If we cannot be united with brothers and sisters who have sinned against us, how can we possibly be united with barbarians who sin against us? Here is good advice:

> Get rid of all bitterness, rage and anger, brawling and slander, along with every form of malice. Be kind and compassionate to one another, forgiving each other, just as in Christ God forgave you. Be imitators of God, therefore, as dearly loved children and live a life of love, just as Christ loved us and gave himself up for us (Ephesians 4:31—5:2).

If a brother sins, we should restore him gently (Galatians 6:1, see also James 5:19, 20), even if he sins against us (Matthew 5:23, 24; 6:12; 18:15-35).

It is easy to talk about forgiveness until we get hurt ourselves. I am convinced that forgiveness is the highest expression of unselfishness. It is the grandest demonstration of dying to self and rising to a newness of life.

Real forgiveness must be coupled with restored fellowship. It is one thing to say, "I'll forgive, but I will never respect that person again and never want to see him again." That is not the forgiveness that Christ offers us. We are to "accept one another, then, just as Christ accepted you" (Romans 15:7). Real forgiveness is seen when the person who has been hurt goes out of his way to serve the needs of the one who has sinned against him. That is what God and Christ have done for us. The Bible

45

is filled with people who became fruitful partly because they forgave others. Sarah forgave Abraham for allowing her to be taken into a king's harem. Esau forgave Jacob for taking the birthright and the blessing of his father away from him. At one time, he declared he wanted to kill Jacob. But the next time they met, he held no grudge and asked for no gift to patch things up. He said, "I already have plenty, my brother. . . . Let us be on our way; I'll accompany you" (Genesis 33:9-12).

Joseph forgave his brothers for hating him, making fun of him, and selling him. He named his two sons after the characteristics that dominated his life and contributed to his success: "God has made me *forget* all my trouble" (Manasseh) and "God has made me *fruitful*" (Ephraim) (Genesis 41:51, 52). Being able to forget the hurts that have been perpetrated against us is directly related to the fruitfulness of our lives.

Forgiving is not easy, but is essential. It should be practiced, first of all, in our homes. More marriages would continue not only through the "better" but also through the "worse" if husbands and wives would forgive each other. More homes would be refuges if parents would forgive children and children would forgive parents.

Sometimes it seems easier to forgive those who are outside the church than those who are in. Our brothers in Christ can hurt us more deeply because they are closer to us. But the privilege of living in Heaven among people who have sinned on earth will be partly determined by our willingness to forgive them—in the here and now.

Why will we be allowed in Heaven at all? It is because of God's grace, mercy, and love that caused Him to forgive us and forget our sins. But the good news of His grace must be expressed by the demonstration of our grace extended to those who sin against us. We can look forward to the Day of Judgment with confidence, but only if we are spreading the good news of forgiveness through our own examples—right now.

Why
Is He Coming Back?
—To Separate

Men have always done a thorough job of separating mankind into different groups. We like to give people labels and put them into groups; then we can treat each one in a certain way according to what group he is in. There are so many labels that separate people that there is no way I can name them all, but here are a few of them: male—female, smart—stupid, management—labor, teacher—student, professional—layman, tall—short, fat—skinny, Jew—Gentile, Westerner—Easterner, beautiful—ugly, Republican—Democrat, Baptist—Methodist (etc.), American—Chinese (etc.), cultured—uncultured, black—white (etc.), primitive—civilized, (etc.).

The Separation

However, when Jesus returns, He will reduce the labeling and divide the entire population of the world into just two groups. This twofold separation is mentioned several times in the New Testament. Let's notice some examples in the teaching of Jesus.

Jesus talked about the separation in the parable of the weeds. Both the good seed and the weeds grew together in the same field until the end of the age. At that time, they were separated into two groups only—not the multitudes of groups that the seeds and the weeds could have been divided into (Matthew 13:24-30, 36-43).

Jesus also talked of the separation in the parable of the net. The net caught all kinds of fish, but they were divided into just two groups (Matthew 13:47-52). Jesus also talked of the two groups in the parable of the sheep and the goats (Matthew 25:31-46).

Jesus implied the separation when He spoke about the two gates (wide and narrow) and the two builders (wise and foolish). He spotlighted two groups of people with two different destinies (Matthew 7:13, 14, 24-27). The New Testament ends with an emphasis upon the two groups—one is saved, while the other is not; one is blessed, while the other is cursed (Revelation 20:11—21:4; 22:14, 15).

Although the final separation will take place formally when Jesus returns, it is taking place functionally even today. Every person in this world is walking on one of two different roads, building on one of two foundations, and thus becoming identified either with the "weeds," "goats," and "bad fish," or with the "good seeds," "sheep," and "good fish."

What decides which group we are in? The ultimate criterion is our identification with Jesus: "He who has the Son has life; he who does not have the Son of God does not have life" (1 John 5:12). But just saying we have the Son does not mean we do. Those who have Jesus will demonstrate His attitude and life-style in their lives.

Some may ask, "If being in Jesus is the true criterion, then why talk about other activities or attitudes? Aren't they superfluous?" No, not at all. When Jesus returns, He will "convict all the ungodly of all the ungodly acts they have done" (Jude 15). If we only pretend to be in

48

Jesus, He will be reminding us on that day of such things as our revengeful spirits and unforgiving attitudes, which are diametrically opposed to being a child of God. When those attitudes and actions are exposed, we will not be able to argue with Him by showing Him our baptismal certificates or church membership rolls.

Being in Christ is not just a position we maintain; it is also a practice we manifest. It is not just a claim backed up by some formal papers or rituals; it is also a character backed up by the way we function. When Jesus returns, He will be looking at our practices and our characters. But we don't have to wait until then to know whether we can support our positions and claims with our practices and characters. In our hearts, we know—unless we have been led to believe that our practices and characters are not important. That is what we are told by the greatest con-artist of all, the devil.

Yes, Jesus makes it clear that He is going to look at something besides our claims on that final day: "Not everyone who says to me, 'Lord, Lord,' will enter the kingdom of heaven, but only he who does the will of my Father who is in heaven" (Matthew 7:21). Jesus will be looking at our faith and our love.

Benevolence

Besides forgiveness, we show our love through our unselfish acts of benevolence, and Jesus made it clear that He will be considering our benevolence when He makes the separation (Matthew 25:31-46). The parable of the sheep and goats was told after a great deal of teaching about the second coming (Matthew 24:1—25:30). Jesus will say to the sheep on His right hand that they will inherit "the kingdom prepared for you since the creation of the world" (Matthew 25:34). Why will the sheep be so blessed?

For I was hungry and you gave me something to eat, I was thirsty and you gave me something to drink, I was a stranger and you invited me in, I needed clothes and you clothed me, I was sick and you looked after me, I was in prison and you came to visit me (Matthew 25:35, 36).

The sheep are unselfish. Humbly they will ask, "Lord, when did we see you hungry and feed you?" (Matthew 25:37-39). They do not know they are helping Jesus. They simply see people in need and help them out of love and compassion. Jesus made the point that whatever is done for or against His people is done for or against Him (Matthew 25:40).

Jesus will send the goats on the left hand "into the eternal fire prepared for the devil and his angels" (Matthew 25:41). Why will the goats be punished?

For I was hungry and you gave me nothing to eat, I was thirsty and you gave me nothing to drink, I was a stranger and you did not invite me in, I needed clothes and you did not clothe me, I was sick and in prison and you did not look after me (Matthew 25:42, 43).

The goats will ask, "Lord, when did we see you hungry or thirsty . . . and did not help you?" (Matthew 25:44). They will be saying, "If we had known it was *You,* we would have done something. We would not neglect *You!*" But Jesus does not succumb to flattery while we are neglecting our fellowmen (Matthew 25:45).

Jesus' final words at the close of the parable reveal to us that our benevolence in the here and now will affect our eternal destiny—"They will go away to eternal punishment, but the righteous to eternal life" (Matthew 25:46).

A student of the New Testament cannot help noticing that Jesus was benevolent while He was on earth. And if we are to live in Him, we must be walking in His sandals and be extending benevolence to those in need. This is a major way that we are to be waiting for the second coming.

Jesus told several other parables that stressed benevolence. The problem with the successful farmer was not that he was wealthy, but that he was selfish with his wealth. He would not share it with those in need (Luke 12:16-21). The problem of the rich man at whose gate Lazarus lay was not that he was rich while another was poor. We will always have distinctions between the rich and poor. God has never been mad at the rich of the world, for no one is richer than God himself. But the trouble lay in the fact that the rich man totally neglected the beggar, Lazarus. He simply did not care that a person was starving to death at his door, so he went to the place of torment (Luke 16:19-31).

The rich man's request that Lazarus be sent to warn his five brothers is interesting. Did he want Lazarus to warn them that there is a place of torment? No, because the Jews believed that. He wanted his brothers to know that they had better start using their possessions to help the poor or they would spend their eternity in torment. That is why the answer was, "If they do not listen to Moses and the Prophets, they will not be convinced even if someone rises from the dead" (Luke 16:31). Moses and the prophets had tons to say about caring for the poor or those in need (just a sampling—Exodus 22:22, 23; 23:11; Leviticus 19:9, 10; Deuteronomy 10:18; 14:28, 29; 15:4-11; Isaiah 1:17; Jeremiah 22:16; Amos 2:6, 7; 5:11, 12; 8:4-7). The rich man's brothers had abundant teaching about being helpful, and so have we! But do we follow the teaching any better than they did?

While waiting for the second coming, every Christian needs to evaluate how he is using his material possessions. Is he using them for himself, or sharing them with those who have physical needs? It is not enough to financially support the ministries that seek to meet spiritual needs (evangelism, teaching, etc.), though they are quite essential. We must also be meeting the physical needs of people. If we don't, our claim that we have the compassionate heart of Jesus will be invalid on the Day of Judgment.

Paul taught that one of the reasons we should work for wages is so that we "may have something to share with those in need" (Ephesians 4:28). But how many of us look at Friday's paycheck with that in mind? Isn't it time every Christian set aside a portion of his income for benevolence? There are too many people around us who are in need for us to ignore them financially. If we cannot be concerned about their lives now, we cannot expect God to be concerned about our lives then.

Part of the structure of the firm foundation upon which we build our lives for eternity is our compassionate benevolence toward others.

> Command those who are rich in this present world not to be arrogant nor to put their hope in wealth, which is so uncertain, but to put their hope in God, who richly provides us with everything for our enjoyment. Command them to do good, to be rich in good deeds, and to be generous and willing to share. In this way they will lay up treasure for themselves as a firm foundation for the coming age, so that they may take hold of the life that is truly life (1 Timothy 6:17-19).

Paul's talk of a firm foundation reminds us of what Jesus said about building on a firm foundation (Matthew 7:24-27).

There is another side to meeting needs or failing to meet them. The Bible's message is not only for those who have material blessings, but also for those who have not. The neglected poor also should wait for the coming of the Savior with proper attitudes and reactions. They must not retaliate against the rich or claim that "what is yours is mine and I will take it." Remember the beggar Lazarus. He was patient and did not complain, and God rewarded him.

James wrote that poor people who were neglected (or cheated out of what they had coming to them) should be patient until the Lord's coming. They should not grumble, but follow the prophets' example of patience in the face of suffering. They should not make rash statements (James 5:1-12).

Indeed both the rich and the poor must check how they are waiting for the Day of Judgment. The poor must not grab or grumble; the rich must care and share.

Why
Is He Coming Back?
—To Unite

On the day that Jesus judges and separates, He will also unite. In fact, He will separate in order to unite. He will separate God's people from those who are without Christ, and then He will unite God's people. Several verses in the Bible stress this point:

> At that time I will tell the harvesters . . . "Gather the wheat and bring it into my barn" (Matthew 13:30).

> Then they sat down and collected the good fish in baskets (Matthew 13:48).

> He will put the sheep on his right (Matthew 25:33).

In each instance, the good people (wheat, good fish, and sheep) are gathered or united together to live as one group for eternity.

Paul spoke of that eternal unity when he wrote the following messages:

> Now there is in store for me the crown of righteousness, which the Lord, the righteous Judge, will award to me on that day—and not only to me, but also to all who have longed for his appearing (2 Timothy 4:8).

> We believe that God will bring with Jesus those who have fallen asleep in him. . . . The dead in Christ will rise first. After that, we who are still alive and are left will be caught up with them in the clouds to meet the Lord in the air. And so we will be with the Lord forever (1 Thessalonians 4:14-17).

After Christ returns, those whose names are written in the book of life will be with the Lord and each other forever (Revelation 7:9-17; 21:1-7, 27; 22:1-5, 14). This unity will cut across all kinds of human distinctions—age, occupation, class, nation, politics, race, gender, geography, denomination, etc. People who belong to human categories that we do not like will be there; they will be there with us forever. That should not shock us, for unity was God's plan before the foundation of the world.

The Plan for Unity

Jesus will return to earth to finalize what He came to initiate the first time He came to earth. He came to put into effect God's scheme to unite all things in Heaven and earth (Ephesians 1:9, 10).

> For God was pleased to have all his fullness dwell in him, and through him to reconcile to himself all things, whether things on earth or things in heaven, by making peace through his blood, shed on the cross (Colossians 1:19, 20).

From the Garden of Eden experience we learned that sin separates man from God and from his fellowmen

(Genesis 3:8, 12, 24; 4:8). We learned that the devil's primary plan is to divide man from God and his fellow-men. Yet even at the separation, God immediately announced His plan to reconcile man both to God himself and to the rest of mankind (Genesis 3:14, 15).

Jesus came into a very disunited world, and He came to bring peace to it (Luke 2:14) by restoring the broken relationships. As Jesus looked the cross in the face, He prayed for the unity that God had planned for and that Jesus would die for:

> My prayer is not for them alone. I pray also for those who will believe in me through their message, that all of them may be one, Father, just as you are in me and I am in you. May they also be in us so that the world may believe that you have sent me. I have given them the glory that you gave me, that they may be one as we are one: I in them and you in me. May they be brought to complete unity to let the world know that you sent me and have loved them even as you have loved me (John 17:20-23).

Jesus then offered himself to die for us. That death is the means of uniting us to God and to each other. Paul expressed this truth:

> But now in Christ Jesus you who once were far away have been brought near through the blood of Christ. For he himself is our peace, who has made the two one and has destroyed the barrier, the dividing wall of hostility, by abolishing in his flesh the law with its commandments and regulations. His purpose was to create in himself one new man out of the two, thus making peace, and in this one body to reconcile both of them to God through the cross, by which he put to death their hostility. He came and preached peace to you who were far away and

peace to those who were near. For through him we both have access to the Father by one Spirit. Consequently, you are no longer foreigners and aliens, but fellow citizens with God's people and members of God's household (Ephesians 2:13-19).

In these verses, Paul was teaching of a restored unity *with God* ("to reconcile both of them to God"; "we both have access to the Father") and *with man* ("fellow citizens with God's people").

A person who is in Christ is united to God (Romans 5:10; Colossians 3:2, 3) and also to others who are in Christ: "There is neither Jew nor Greek, slave nor free, male nor female, for you are all one in Christ Jesus" (Galatians 3:28). This was the type of reconciliation that Paul wrote about:

All this is from God, who reconciled us to himself through Christ. . . . God was reconciling the world to himself in Christ, not counting men's sins against them (2 Corinthians 5:18, 19).

Jesus went to the cross to unite us and will return to gather God's people together in a united group that will live together throughout all eternity. What should we be doing in the meantime? We must be practicing unity in our lives right now.

The Practice of Unity

One of the things that grieved Paul's heart was the way God's people were living with hostilities toward fellow Christians. He wrote every letter to the churches partly to help teach the Christians how to live in unity while waiting for the second coming. He made it clear that Christians should live for one another in spite of earthly distinctions or differences of opinion (Romans 12—16), that Christians in one geographical location were united with saints in every other location (1 Corinthians 1:2), and that all things should be done for building up the earthly body of Christ—the church (1 Corinthians 12—14). He even wrote that if any one destroys the unity of the church (the body of Christ), God will destroy him (1 Corinthians 3:16, 17). He emphasized that it was harmful to take the Lord's Supper while harboring factious attitudes (1 Corinthians 11:17-34).

Bringing disunity into the church is so opposed to the correct way of living that Paul wrote that the divisive person should be expelled from the church after a second warning (Titus 3:10). Why take such a drastic action? Because such a person demonstrates that he stands opposed to the very purpose of Christ's coming. Such a person is trying to undo God's plan for unity that was announced in the Garden of Eden. Such a person is "warped and sinful" (Titus 3:11). Paul wrote that we should keep away from those who cause divisions (Romans 16:17).

God has not given to us the spirit of dissension, but the Holy Spirit, whose fruit maintains unity:

> But the fruit of the Spirit is love, joy, peace, patience, kindness, goodness, faithfulness, gentleness and self-control. Against such things there is no law. Those who belong to Christ Jesus have crucified the sinful nature with its passion and desires. Since we live by the Spirit, let us keep in step with the Spirit. Let us not become conceited, provoking and envying each other (Galatians 5:22-26).

When that Holy Spirit is given to us as we die with Christ and rise to a new life (Romans 6), we are also given the ministry of reconciliation (2 Corinthians 5:18-20). One of the characteristics of the "new creation" is that we live to restore relationships, not to fracture them (2 Corinthians 5:17).

If we are going to anticipate unity with all of God's people on the day Christ returns, we had better be living lives of unity now. Hasn't God had enough of the way Christians backbite one another, hold grudges. and ignore those of another group? Hasn't God seen enough competition among Christians who ought to be cooperating? Hasn't He seen enough of His children being treated like enemies instead of loving family members? Hasn't He seen enough divisions and heartaches caused by differences of opinion? We are to live *for* and *with* the body of Christ—which includes *all* the members of that body. We must be living demonstrations of the reconciliation that Jesus Christ brought into reality.

We are given a mandate to "make every effort to keep the unity of the Spirit through the bond of peace" (Ephesians 4:3). How do we do that? By recognizing our unity amid our different human characteristics and abilities (Ephesians 4:7-16), and by our personal conduct with others.

Our conduct should include the following:

1. Controlling our anger (Ephesians 4:26).
2. Working to help the needy (Ephesians 4:28).
3. Speaking to help, not hurt (Ephesians 4:29).
4. Getting rid of malice (Ephesians 4:31).
5. Being kind and forgiving (Ephesians 4:32).
6. Living in harmony with others (Romans 12:14-16).
7. Not retaliating when wronged (Romans 12:17-21).
8. Accepting different opinions (Romans 14:1-23).
9. Not dividing (1 Corinthians 1—4).
10. Being willing to be cheated rather than to take advantage of another (1 Corinthians 6:1-8).
11. Helping restore fellowship between those who differ (Philippians 4:2, 3).
12. Obeying our leaders (Hebrews 13:7, 17).
13. Living moral lives (Ephesians 5:3-20).
14. Orderly family life (Ephesians 5:22—6:4).

In short, the Christian is to be committed to live for others (Romans 15:1-3). Anything short of that will eventually breed disunity. That is why we read of so many ways in the New Testament that we are to treat each other. Here is a partial list:

1. Be devoted to one another (Romans 12:10).
2. Live in harmony with one another (Romans 12:16).
3. Love one another (Romans 13:8).
4. Refrain from judging one another (Romans 14:13).
5. Edify one another (Romans 14:19).
6. Accept one another (Romans 15:7).
7. Instruct one another (Romans 15:14).
8. Greet one another (Romans 16:16).
9. Care for one another (1 Corinthians 12:25).
1p. Serve one another (Galatians 5:13).
11. Bear one another's burdens (Galatians 6:2).
12. Forgive one another (Ephesians 4:32).
13. Submit to one another (Ephesians 5:21).
14. Encourage one another (Hebrews 3:13).
15. Offer hospitality to one another (1 Peter 4:9).
16. Fellowship with one another (1 John 1:7).

We will be living with one another forever; let us start practicing unity now. Of course, merely maintaining unity among ourselves is not enough. We must await the second coming in such a way that we become instruments through whom unity with others is created. That means we are to be Christ's ambassadors "as though God were making his appeal through us. We implore you on Christ's behalf: Be reconciled to God" (2 Corinthians 5:20). We evangelize to unite—to unite others with God and with their fellowmen (1 John 1:3).

When that gathering of unity happens, may we be ready to join the group of God's saints because we are living to maintain and initiate unity in the here and now.

Why
Is He Coming Back?
—To Condemn

When Jesus returns, "there will be a resurrection of both the righteous and the wicked" (Acts 24:15). However, being resurrected will not be good news for everyone. Some will rise to live, but others will rise to be condemned (John 5:29).

The Reality of Condemnation

Several Bible verses tell of this condemnation:

First collect the weeds and tie them in bundles to be burned (Matthew 13:30).

The Son of Man will send out his angels, and they will weed out of his kingdom everything that causes sin and all who do evil. They will throw them into the fiery furnace, where there will be weeping and gnashing of teeth (Matthew 13:41, 42).

The angels will come and separate the wicked from the righteous and throw them into the fiery furnace, where there will be weeping and gnashing of teeth (Matthew 13:49, 50).

Then the king told the attendants, "Tie him hand and foot, and throw him outside, into the darkness" (Matthew 22:13).

And throw that worthless servant outside, into the darkness, where there will be weeping and gnashing of teeth (Matthew 25:30).

Then he will say to those on his left, Depart from me, you who are cursed, into the eternal fire prepared for the devil and his angels (Matthew 25:41).

But he will reply, "I don't know you or where you come from. Away from me, all you evildoers! (Luke 13:27).

The rich man also died and was buried. In hell, where he was in torment . . . (Luke 16:22, 23).

If anyone destroys God's temple, God will destroy him (1 Corinthians 3:17).

Many live as enemies of the cross of Christ. Their destiny is destruction . . . (Philippians 3:18, 19).

He will punish those who do not know God and do not obey the gospel of our Lord Jesus. They will be punished with everlasting destruction and shut out from the presence of the Lord and from the majesty of his power (2 Thessalonians 1:8, 9).

The present heavens and earth are reserved for fire, being kept for the day of judgment and destruction of ungodly men (2 Peter 3:7).

If anyone worships the beast and his image . . . he too will drink of the wine of God's fury, which has been poured full strength into the cup of his wrath. He will be tormented with burning sulfur in the presence of the holy angels and of the Lamb. And the smoke of their torment rises for ever and ever (Revelation 14:9-11).

And the devil, who deceived them, was thrown into the lake of burning sulfur, where the beast and the false prophet had been thrown. They will be tormented day and night for ever and ever (Revelation 20:10).

And I saw the dead, great and small, standing before the throne, and books were opened. Another book was opened, which is the book of life. The dead were judged according to what they had done as recorded in the books. The sea gave up the dead that were in it, and death and Hades gave up the dead that were in them, and each person was judged according to what he had done. Then death and Hades were thrown into the lake of fire. The lake of fire is the second death. If anyone's name was not found written in the book of life, he was thrown into the lake of fire (Revelation 20:12-15).

But the cowardly, the unbelieving, the vile, the murderers, the sexually immoral, those who practice magic arts, the idolaters and all liars—their place will be in the fiery lake of burning sulfur. This is the second death (Revelation 21:8).

The Reason for Condemnation

As we read the Scriptures, we can understand that without a doubt God will condemn some on Judgment Day. But that does not mean that God delights in condemning anyone. We must understand the balance of God's activity. The flip side of condemnation is salvation. In nearly every passage of Scripture quoted above, salvation is mentioned with almost the same breath as condemnation. Salvation is what God does for man, while condemnation is what man does to himself.

It would be easy to read about condemnation and then ask, "How can a God of love allow that? How can a God be just who allows that?" Here are some facts that each person must consider before saying God is unjust:

1. Man's sin brought devastation to God's creation. The beauty and harmony of the original creation became miserably altered by sin. All the terribleness that the earth has experienced was ushered in by man's rebellious selfishness. Man deserves to be punished.

2. Every person deserves condemnation, for "the wages of sin is death" (Romans 6:23) and "all have sinned" (Romans 3:23). "There is no one righteous, not even one" (Romans 3:10). So rather than complain that God will condemn some, we should be thankful that He will save some.

3. God has been "above board" in communicating to man about eternal destinies. He has openly revealed himself and His plan for salvation for all. He sent Jesus to save us from our sins (Matthew 1:21).

4. God loves man. Sending Jesus to take man's condemnation upon himself proves that. Jesus carried man's sins to the cross (Isaiah 53:4-6; 1 Peter 2:22-24; Hebrews 2:9). God sacrificed His child for those who were His enemies. How would you like to try that?

5. God does not desire that *anyone* perish. In fact, He has delayed the return of Jesus to give more people time to repent (2 Peter 3:9).

6. God has commissioned the church to evangelize the world (Matthew 28:19, 20). The gospel of Jesus Christ is the power of God for salvation for everyone who believes (Romans 1:16).

7. Because of the grace of God, man can choose not to be condemned.

8. But if man decides that he does not want to change his earthly commitments and his eternal destiny, God does not force His will on anyone. God will give man up to his own desires (Romans 1:24, 26, 28).

9. A person who is miserable on earth with God's life-style and with God's people would be miserable in Heaven. God will not permit the selfish and rebellious to enter Heaven and bring to it the chaos, the bitterness, the hatred, and the wars that they bring to the earth.

10. The condemnation of sin is counterbalanced by the grace of forgiveness. In fact, "where sin increased, grace increased all the more" (Romans 5:20).

11. God does not judge anyone with a prejudiced or unjust mind (Revelation 16:7; 19:2).

12. Man is not condemned *at* the second coming; he is condemned *prior* to that day by his own sin. Unless he accepts God's life preserver—Jesus—he is condemned already (John 3:18). The Day of Judgment will be the announcement of that condemnation in such a way that the convicted will understand that they deserve their destiny (Jude 14, 15).

God is not holding grudges and is not anxiously awaiting the time when He can pounce down upon man. On the final day God will be merely announcing what man has chosen for himself. Though man's choice will not please God, He allows man to make the choice (Romans 1:24, 26, 28). What condemns man is sin.

The Responsibilities of the Saved

In light of the fact that those outside of Christ are condemned already, what should the saved be doing as they await the second coming?

The saved should be evangelizing the lost. If God does not want one single person to perish, then God's children should share that attitude and back it up with the actions of evangelism. It is a strange phenomenon that some Christians seem elated by the fact that many will be condemned. Some talk about it almost with a smile on their faces. The reality of condemnation should never give a Christian joy. No Christian should ever look at the condemned and say, "I thank God that I am not like him." Instead the Christian should pray, "By the grace of God I am what I am, and I want him to share that grace."

Evangelism calls for many different activities. We must share the good news by our words, for faith comes by hearing (Romans 10:13-17). God expects us to share the words by which a man can be saved (Acts 11:14). To leave that type of speaking to the professional preacher is to show we lack compassion and to functionally deny what Jesus came to do—to seek and save the lost (Luke 19:10). Claiming that people would rather "see a sermon" than hear one, some Christians try to be do-gooders without speaking of Jesus. This is a cop-out. Unless we share the good news in words, people will not know why we do good. However, effective evangelism does also require living Christlike lives so people can see Christ through us.

Effective evangelism also requires unity (John 17:20, 21) and the edification of new Christians, who are babes in Christ (1 Peter 2:2). Teaching them helps to insure their stability and maturity. It also enables them to better evangelize others.

There is also something Christians should *not* be doing as they await Jesus' return. We are not to be condemning people before that final day. We are to share the Word of God and let the Holy Spirit "convict the world of guilt in regard to sin and righteousness and judgment" (John 16:8).

Sometimes Christians are too prone to act as judge, jury, and executioner. Paul wrote, "Therefore judge nothing before the appointed time; wait till the Lord comes. He will bring to light what is hidden in darkness and will expose the motives of men's hearts" (1 Corinthians 4:5). This does not mean that we are not to call sin by its right name. We are (1 Corinthians 5). Nor does it mean that we are not to make judgments that can help Christians solve disputes. We are (1 Corinthians 6). Nor does it mean that we are not to admonish the erring brother. We are (2 Thessalonians 3:14, 15; Galatians 6:1; James 5:19, 20). But it does mean that we are to recognize that the *final* judgment belongs to Jesus (John 5:27). He will allow some Christians to participate in the judgment (Matthew 19:28; 1 Corinthians 6:2), but none is to do such judging ahead of time. Until that final day, we are to be ministers of reconciliation by taking the remedy for sin to sinful men (2 Corinthians 5:17-21).

In short, we have no right ever to give up on a person or to throw up our hands in disgust and walk away from him. To do that is to condemn him ahead of time.

At the final condemnation, we will see what God meant when He said, "It is mine to avenge; I will repay" (Romans 12:19; Hebrews 10:30). To recognize that vengeance is the Lord's is to wait for the second coming without seeking for personal revenge.

> Do not repay anyone evil for evil. Be careful to do what is right in the eyes of everybody. If it is possible, as far as it depends on you, live at peace with everyone. Do not take revenge, my friends, but leave room for God's wrath, for it is written: "It is mine to avenge; I will repay," says the Lord. On the contrary: "If your enemy is hungry, feed him; if he is thirsty, give him something to drink. In doing this, you will heap burning coals on his head." Do not be overcome by evil, but overcome evil with good (Romans 12:17-21).

Living without condemning another and without seeking revenge while we are busy evangelizing—this is what we must be doing as we await the Christ.

Why

Is He Coming Back?

—To Commend

Jesus is coming back not only to pass out condemnation, but also to pass out commendation. For God's people, the return of Jesus will be the greatest day on earth. It will be a day of victory, not defeat; a day of joy, not grief; a day of blessing, not cursing; a day of comfort, not affliction; a day of inheritance, not bankruptcy; a day of eternal life, not eternal death; a day of being confessed, not being denied; a day of rewards, not retribution; a day of approval, not disapproval; a day of glory, not shame; a day of God's wonder, not wrath; a day of rest, not pressure. It will be a "great day" of wrath for the wicked, (Jude 6, Revelation 6:17) but a great day filled with glorious experiences for the persons whose lives are united with God through Jesus Christ.

A Day of Confession

Not only will we confess Jesus as Lord on that final day, but Jesus will also acknowledge us before the Heavenly Father and the angels of God. He made that promise plain.

> Whoever acknowledges me before men, I will also acknowledge him before my Father in heaven (Matthew 10:32).

> I tell you, whoever acknowledges me before men, the Son of Man will also acknowledge him before the angels of God (Luke 12:8).

It is probably not possible to fathom the thrill that Jesus' confession will give to us. Yesterday I received a personal invitation in the mail from the inaugural committee to attend the inauguration ceremony and ball of the next Missouri governor. Imagine what a thrill it would be if the governor stopped part of the inaugural proceedings or the ball, waited for silence and the attention of all those present, and then turned to me and announced that he wanted to acknowledge me, Knofel Staton. And even have me stand up! Of course that will not happen.

But there will be the even greater thrill of having the Governor of all governors personally and publicly acknowledge each one of us by name. He will single you out for personal recognition. There will be no such thing as God's unknown servants who hide in the woodwork. You may be unknown now, but you will be known to all then. Everyone will know you by name! What a day that will be!

We have this thrill to look forward to, but we must not forget that Jesus is right now "going to bat" for us before the almighty God. "But if anybody does sin, we have one who speaks to the Father in our defense—Jesus Christ, the Righteous One" (1 John 2:1). The devil keeps a record of all the wrong we have done or thought and accuses us before the Father night and day (Revelation 12:10), but Jesus "runs interference" for those who are His.

This compassionate action of Jesus should cause us to acknowledge Him before men in the here and now. If the perfect one is not ashamed to confess us who are imperfect before the holy God, then we should feel no hesitancy or shame to confess Him before unholy men. In fact, our activity of confession in His earthly campaign is a must if we expect Him to acknowledge us on that day.

A Day of Commendation

He will not only mention our names for all to hear on that day; He will also reveal to everyone all that we have done for Him. Although He will forget our sins, He will remember our services. What grace! Have you ever felt that no one really knows what you are doing for God because most of your activities are "behind the scenes"? It may be to your advantage that others do not know, because it is so easy to begin doing good deeds for the human response and applause.

Jesus spoke of hypocrites who had a "grandstand" type of religion, and the only reward they would get would be from men who applauded them (Matthew 6:1-4). We must all be careful about serving for the praise of others. Such seeking for earthly recognition may dilute the thrill we will have when God praises us on that great day. Some people even hid their faith in Jesus because "they loved praise from men more than praise from God" (John 12:43).

Whatever good you have done behind the scenes will be put in center stage when Jesus returns (Matthew 6:4). God's servants will receive praise for what they have done, just as Paul promised: "At that time each will receive his praise from God" (1 Corinthians 4:5).

But in order to receive commendation on that day, we must make an effort now "to obtain the praise that comes from the only God" (John 5:44). We must be like the servants who anticipated the return of their master and lived so the master would be pleased with them when he did return. Such actions preceded the coveted declaration, "Well done, good and faithful servant!" (Matthew 25:14-23).

A Day of Universal Reward

The confession and commendation from Jesus will be accompanied by the rewarding of His servants. Jesus has an award for "all who have longed for his appearing" (2 Timothy 4:8). The reward is summed up in the phrase "eternal life," but has many specific facets included in it. Here are a few:

1. *A crown.* A crown is given to winners. The Christian's crown is referred to in different ways in the Bible:

a. "A crown that will last forever" (1 Corinthians 9:25). It is not a temporary possession that someone can take away from us, nor will it fade with time, like the laurel wreath awarded to a winner in the Corinthian games. It is not only a symbol of being a winner, but also a symbol of royalty. We will be crowned and reign with Christ (2 Timothy 2:12).

b. "The crown of righteousness" (2 Timothy 4:8). Here and now we try to be righteous, but we succeed only because Jesus takes away our sins and gives us His righteousness instead. The crowning righteousness will be ours when we become as Jesus (1 John 3:2).

c. "The crown of glory" (1 Peter 5:4). Here and now we live to glorify God (Matthew 5:16), but at Christ's coming we shall share His glory (Colossians 3:4).

d. "The crown of life" (James 1:12; Revelation 2:10). Jesus will crown us with eternal life. Death will not follow us to Heaven.

2. *An inheritance.* Paul wrote, "You will receive an inheritance from the Lord as a reward" (Colossians 3:24). What will we inherit as "heirs of God and co-heirs with Christ"? (Romans 8:17). We will share in all that is God's, and He owns everything. We will become joint owners of the new heaven and the new earth (Matthew 5:3, 5; 2 Peter 3:13). It is no wonder that the Bible says that he who gains this whole temporary world and loses his own soul has made a bad trade (Matthew 16:26). Our inheritance is being kept in Heaven for us (1 Peter 1:4),

which means it is quite secure. It will never perish, spoil, or fade.

3. *The right to eat from the tree of life.* Whatever Adam and Eve lost by being separated from the tree of life, we will gain as a reward (Revelation 2:7; 22:2, 14).

4. *The hidden manna* (Revelation 2:17). Elsewhere we learn that Jesus himself is the bread from Heaven (John 6:35, 48-51). Our reward will include continuous fellowship with Jesus on a personal basis with all the benefits that come with it.

5. *A white stone* (Revelation 2:17). A white stone was given to victors (we will be winners), to the acquitted (we will not be declared guilty), to those freed from slavery (we will be liberated), and to those warriors who returned victorious from a battle (we will have fought the good fight and won).

6. *A new name* (Revelation 2:17; 3:12). The new name will be the name of the divine God and His Son and the new Jerusalem. A new name means a new status. In fact, all things will be made new (Revelation 21:5).

7. *Authority over the nations* (Revelation 2:26). Christians will share in the judgment of the nations.

8. *The morning star* (Revelation 2:28). The morning star is Jesus (Revelation 22:16). We will be ushered into His presence to remain with Him forever.

9. *A pillar in the temple of God* (Revelation 3:12). We will never have to fear that we will have to leave the presence of God—not even for a second.

A Day of Individualized Rewards

Jesus will reward *all* His people (as we discussed in the foregoing paragraphs); but the New Testament also teaches that rewards will be individualized.

The idea of different rewards may bother us because competition in this world sometimes is unfriendly. But in Heaven there will be no jealousy or envy due to differences in the rewards that are handed out. We will be transformed into Christlikeness (1 John 3:2). We will not be jealous of anyone else, even though someone may get a higher degree of reward than we do. Jealousy is a mark of spiritual immaturity (1 Corinthians 3:1-4), but in Heaven we will be mature. Pure love will exist in Heaven; and love "does not envy, it does not boast, it is not proud. It is not rude, it is not self-seeking . . ." (1 Corinthians 13:4, 5). "If one part is honored, every part rejoices with it" (1 Corinthians 12:26) whenever we love properly. Rewards may be different, but each person will be happy with his own reward because it will be specially suited to him.

The following Scriptures indicate that there will be individualized rewards:

Anyone who receives a prophet because he is a prophet will receive a prophet's reward, and anyone who receives a righteous man because he is a righteous man will receive a righteous man's reward. And if anyone gives a cup of cold water to one of these little ones because he is my disciple, I tell you the truth, he will certainly not lose his reward (Matthew 10:41, 42).

"Well done, my good servant," his master replied. "Because you have been trustworthy in a very small matter, take charge of ten cities." . . . "You take charge of five cities" (Luke 19:17-19).

The man who plants and the man who waters have one purpose, and each will be rewarded according to his own labor (1 Corinthians 3:8).

What to Do Now

Notice that the rewards that are mentioned are connected with earthly responsibilities—being hospitable to God's spokesmen, being responsible with small assignments, and carrying out commissioned labors. We are not to sit around and wait to be rewarded. Special rewards result from special activities.

Expecting different rewards in Heaven, how should we be living now on earth? We should be living in harmony with Christians who are receiving more rewards on earth than we are, also with those who are receiving less. We should not feel either superior or inferior, but we should realize that we are members of one another and live with mutual helpfulness (1 Corinthians 12:12-31). We should honor one another rather than ourselves (Romans 12:10). We should "do nothing out of selfish ambition or vain conceit." In humility we should consider others better than ourselves (Philippians 2:3). We should rejoice when a fellow member is honored (1 Corinthians 12:26) and not brood because we are not so honored. We should be happy with our differing lots on earth as we will be with our differing rewards in Heaven.

When Jesus comes He will "give to everyone according to what he has done" (Revelation 22:12). We will all share in the universal rewards, and we will rejoice sincerely if Jesus gives to others some honors that we don't receive. We will be happy with what He gives to us, for we will see that it is truly right for us.

Yes, the return of Jesus will be a great day for His people. Let us be prepared by putting away jealousy, envy, and unfriendly competition. Let us put on simple servanthood.

Why
Is He Coming Back?

—To Transform

On that final day, Jesus will come to change us. In what way? He will change us bodily.

Many people wonder if we will have bodies in Heaven. The answer is yes, but they will be different from our earthly bodies. When Jesus returns, He will transform these bodies of ours. Paul taught about that bodily transformation:

> But our citizenship is in heaven. And we eagerly await a Savior from there, the Lord Jesus Christ, who, by the power that enables him to bring everything under his control, will transform our lowly bodies so that they will be like his glorious body (Philippians 3:20, 21).

The Fact

The question that the people asked in Paul's day is still a popular question: "With what kind of body will they come?" (1 Corinthians 15:35). Sometimes the thought behind the question is this: "How can a person have a body that is different in kind from what he now has and still be the same person?

Paul answered that question for the Corinthians with the following points:

1. The earthly body is related to the transformed body in a way similar to the way a seed is related to the plant that grows from it. The plant is not the same as the seed, but the seed is a necessary prelude to the plant (1 Corinthians 15:36, 37).

2. God will give us the kind of body that He determines (1 Corinthians 15:38).

3. As there are different kinds of bodies on earth (animals, birds, fish, etc.), the bodies in Heaven and the bodies on earth are different. The body of a person on earth is different from the body of the same person in Heaven (1 Corinthians 15:39-41).

4. The resurrected body will be different from the earthly body in many ways as they are plainly stated(1 Corinthians 15:42-50).

Earthly	**Heavenly**
perishable	imperishable
dishonored	honored
weak	powerful
natural	spiritual
like Adam	like Christ
from dust	from Heaven

The change will be so significant that in Heaven our bodies will not experience tears, death, mourning, crying, pain (Revelation 21:4). There will be faultless fellowship, but no marriage (Matthew 22:30). God will make everything new (Revelation 21:5).

5. The change will happen with certainty. "Listen, I tell you a mystery: We will not all sleep, but we will all be changed" (1 Corinthians 15:51).

6. The change will happen quickly—"in a flash, in the twinkling of an eye, at the last trumpet. For the trumpet will sound, the dead will be raised imperishable, and we will be changed" (1 Corinthians 15:52).

7. The change is essential if we are to live in Heaven, for "flesh and blood cannot inherit the kingdom of God" (1 Corinthians 15:50); "the perishable must clothe itself with the imperishable, and the mortal with immortality" (1 Corinthians 15:53).

8. The transformation will be the primary signal of victory for God's people: "When the perishable has been clothed with the imperishable, and the mortal with immortality, then the saying that is written will come true: 'Death has been swallowed up in victory' " (1 Corinthians 15:54).

9. The transformation has these results: fulfills prophecy (1 Corinthians 15:54; Isaiah 25:8), brings victory over death (1 Corinthians 15:55), brings victory over sin and the law (1 Corinthians 15:56), completes the purpose of Jesus' sacrifice (1 Corinthians 15:57), causes us to be thankful to God for Jesus (1 Corinthians 15:57), and motivates us to give ourselves fully to the work of the Lord, knowing that our labor in the Lord is not in vain (1 Corinthians 15:58).

This last point is crucial to us, for it gives us insight about how to wait for the second coming. If we want God to change our bodies then, we should make changes in our lives now. Paul put it this way: "Therefore, I urge you, brothers, in view of God's mercy, to offer your bodies as living sacrifices holy and pleasing to God." (Romans 12:1).

We can give ourselves in this way as we apply the fourfold formula of the early church to our lives: "They devoted themselves to the apostles' teaching and to the fellowship, to the breaking of bread and to prayer" (Acts 2:42). Each one of these activities involves giving ourselves both to God and to our fellowmen.

While the first (apostles' doctrine) involves listening to God speaking through men, the last one (prayer) involves talking to God on behalf of men. And as we listen and pray, we fellowship and break bread with God and our fellowmen. Fellowship and the breaking of bread involve more than social events and worship time; they include sharing our lives in service to both God and man. Such service calls for unselfishness that is hard to achieve. But that is the way we are to live as we look forward to God's transformation of our bodies to a Heavenly existence.

By living unselfishly we are bringing to earth a bit of Heavenly living. We allow the church to be a colony of Heaven on earth. Paul made that application in the first fourteen chapters of 1 Corinthians. He said Christians were not to be divided over human leaders (chapters 1-4); they were to stop immorality (5:1-8); they were to be involved in the world (5:9-12); they were not to take advantage of fellow Christians or have the attitude of "I want what's coming to me" (6:1-11); they were to flee from sexual immorality (6:12-20); they were to take their marriages seriously and fulfill the responsibilities of them (chapter 7); they were not to fuss over matters of opinion, but be willing to yield their rights (chapters 8-10); they were to stop confusion during worship (11:2-16); they were to live in harmony with fellow Christians (11:17-34); they were to use God's gifts to serve one another, not to compete against each other (chapters 12-14).

Each of these actions demands that we love unselfishly and that we put our own desires on the back burner. We must look out for others. I know what the best selling books say: "Pull your own strings" and "Look out for number one." Is it really worth it to live in God's way instead of the world's way of looking out for self only? Yes, it is worth it because of the glorious transformation that awaits us.

> Therefore, my dear brothers, stand firm. Let nothing move you. Always give yourselves fully to the work of the Lord, because you know that your labor in the Lord is not in vain (1 Corinthians 15:58).

Christ will not transform just our bodies; He will also transform our attitudes. Our total selves will change. John revealed that when he wrote:

> Dear friends, now we are children of God, and what we will be has not yet been made known. But we know that when he appears, we shall be like him, for we shall see him as he is (1 John 3:2).

God has always wanted to change our sinful selves. His goal has always been that we become like Jesus: "For those God foreknew he also predestined to be conformed to the likeness of his son . . ." (Romans 8:29). See also 1 John 3:2.

The Beginning

The second coming of Christ will not commence the tranformation, but will climax it. The transformation begins when we become a "new creation" (2 Corinthians 5:17) at the time of our first resurrection. That first resurrection happens when, as the result of faith and repentance, we are buried with Christ in baptism. We are then raised with Him to a newness of life that begins in the here and now.

Having been buried with him in baptism and raised with him through your faith in the power of God, who raised him from the dead. When you were dead in your sins and in the uncircumcision of your sinful nature, God made you alive with Christ. He forgave us all our sins (Colossians 2:12, 13).

We were therefore buried with him through baptism into death in order that, just as Christ was raised from the dead through the glory of the Father, we too may live a new life (Romans 6:4).

You are all sons of God through faith in Christ Jesus, for all of you who were baptized into Christ have been clothed with Christ (Galatians 3:26, 27).

Therefore, if anyone is in Christ, he is a new creation; the old has gone, the new has come! (2 Corinthians 5:17).

The Process

The person in Christ has been born again (John 3:1-21) through renewal by the Holy Spirit (Titus 3:5). That spirit is God's nature who lives within us in order to empower us to be daily changing and maturing into the likeness of Christ. As newborn babes we are to grow. We are to be in the daily process of transformation.

Like newborn babies, crave pure spiritual milk, so that by it you may grow up in your salvation, now that you have tasted that the Lord is good (1 Peter 2:2, 3).

And we, who with unveiled faces all reflect the Lord's glory, are being transformed into his likeness with ever-increasing glory, which comes from the Lord, who is the Spirit (2 Corinthians 3:18).

Instead, speaking the truth in love, we will in all things grow up into him who is the Head, that is, Christ (Ephesians 4:15).

God has already started the process of transformation in us; thus we have a mandate from Him to show it by a commitment to change:

You were taught, with regard to your former way of life, to put off your old self, which is being corrupted by its deceitful desires; to be made new in the attitude of your minds; and to put on the new self, created to be like God in true righteousness and holiness (Ephesians 4:22-24).

Since we live by the Spirit, let us keep in step with the Spirit (Galatians 5:25).

In the same way, count yourselves dead to sin but alive to God in Christ Jesus. Therefore do not let sin reign in your mortal body so that you obey its evil desires. Do not offer the parts of your body to sin, as instruments of wickedness, but rather offer yourselves to God, as those who have been brought from death to life; and offer the parts of your body to him as instruments of righteousness (Romans 6:11-13).

Do not conform any longer to the pattern of this world, but be transformed by the renewing of your mind. Then you will be able to test and approve what God's will is—his good, pleasing and perfect will (Romans 12:2).

Since then, you have been raised with Christ, set your hearts on things above, where Christ is seated at the right hand of God. Set your minds on things above, not on earthly things. You . . . have put on the new self, which is being renewed in knowledge in the image of its Creator (Colossians 3:1, 2, 10).

John made it clear that if we hope to become like Jesus in the climaxing stage of the transformation, we will begin to be like Him on earth now: "Everyone who has this hope in him purifies himself, just as he is pure" (1 John 3:3).

Waiting for the second coming is not to be a passive, rocking-chair existence, nor are we to simply stand around looking into the clouds. It involves imitating Jesus in how we act, think, and react (Ephesians 5:1; 1 Corinthians 11:1). From baptism on, our waiting is a lifetime of transformation. Are you being transformed now? Are you becoming like Christ daily?

A Look Above

It is not always easy to wait for the second coming in the ways that we should, because life on earth is often very difficult. Life can be filled with so many problems that we may be tempted to say, "Stop the world; I want to get off!" Paul expressed some of that type of frustration when he wrote, "I desire to depart and be with Christ, which is better by far" (Philippians 1:23), and, "We are confident, I say, and would prefer to be away from the body and at home with the Lord" (2 Corinthians 5:8). Thinking about our own future life with Jesus, we can understand Paul's preference.

Although Paul vented his frustration, he never lost sight of the practical view: "It is more necessary for you that I remain in the body" (Philippians 1:24). Christ did not create the church just so her members could go to Heaven. He created the church so she could help life on earth be different and of a higher quality by her penetration into the world as light, leaven, salt, the body of Christ, the children of God, servants, branches, ambassadors, etc.

At the same time, that does not mean that life for Christians is a "bowl of cherries" or a "rose garden." At times, life may give us the thorns and throw away the roses, or life may be the "pits" with no cherries. Paul knew what it meant to wait for Jesus' return in the midst of rough times:

For it seems to me that God has put us apostles on display at the end of the procession, like men condemned to die in the arena. We have been made a spectacle to the whole universe, to angels as well as to men. We are fools for Christ . . . we are weak . . . we are dishonored . . . we go hungry and thirsty, we are in rags, we are brutally treated, we are homeless. We work hard with our hands . . . we are cursed . . . we are persecuted . . . we are slandered . . . we have become the scum of the earth, the refuse of the world (1 Corinthians 4:9-13).

I have worked much harder, been in prison more frequently, been flogged more severely, and been exposed to death again and again. Five times I received from the Jews the forty lashes minus one. Three times I was beaten with rods, once I was stoned, three times I was shipwrecked, I spent a night and a day in the open sea, I have been constantly on the move. I have been in danger from rivers, in danger from bandits, in danger from my own countrymen, in danger from Gentiles; in danger in the city, in danger in the country, in danger at sea; and in danger from false brothers. I have labored and toiled and have often gone without sleep; I have known hunger and thirst and have often gone without food; I have been cold and naked. Besides everything else, I face daily the pressure of my concern for all the churches (2 Corinthians 11:23-28).

Other early Christians also knew about tough times as they waited for Jesus to return. By the end of the first century, they were experiencing pressure from every angle. On the one hand, intellectualism (Gnosticism) was telling them they were wrong. On the other hand, governmental policies were treating them as if they were wrong.

They were being bombarded mentally by the educators and physically by the emperors. Christians who did not bow down in the worship of the emperor and confess him as "God, Savior, and Lord" were tortured, deported, and executed. Some were dipped in tar and attached to posts that surrounded the athletic arena; then they were set on fire and became living "flood lights" for the evening games. On several occasions, Christians became the main attraction at the arena, for they were put inside fresh animal skins and placed in the center of the arena for the wild animals and dogs to chew on. The spectators cheered as the Christians were torn apart.

In addition to all of that, nature seemed to be giving them a rough time—famine and disease were common (Acts 11:27-30). And to top it all off, problems from within the church itself threatened the well-being of Christians. Christian brothers turned against each other in their doctrines and deeds (Revelation 2 and 3).

In the midst of these many problems, some Christians were asking understandable questions: "Why, God? Have we chosen the right God after all? Where are You, God? Don't You care about what is happening to us? Are You really the powerful Lord we have always thought You were, or is the emperor the real power on earth?" I'm sure each one of us asks those same questions in some form or another as the problems bombard us while Jesus delays His coming.

It is essential for us to maintain a proper perspective as we wait for the Lord to come in the midst of our present crises. Our perspective should be threefold: (a) a looking above, (b) a looking inside, (c) a looking ahead. John led the people of his day to understand these three perspectives.

Who's In Charge?

Before dealing with the problems the Christians were facing, John told them to "look above." He knew they needed to see God as He was, lest they become hoodwinked into believing the emperor. We also need to see God as He is, lest the powerful forces on earth cause us to look in the wrong direction for our leader.

John heard that Jesus is the first and the last, the Alpha and Omega. He is in control regardless of how desperate things seem. He and the Father are still alive and on the throne. No one can kick them around. The one who was is the same one who is, and He is coming back (Revelation 1:8; 22:12, 13). He is not on the same level as any earthly ruler, for He is the ruler of all the kings of the earth (Revelation 1:5). No one will ever have veto power over God or Jesus.

Where Are You, Lord?

But if God is so powerful, why is He allowing His people to go through such tough times? Is God on vacation? No, Jesus is absent from the earth, but He is not gone. Although He is coming back in a visible way, He is still very much on earth now in His Spirit. He left promising to be with us (Matthew 28:20), and we are told that He lives in each of us (John 14:18-23; 1 Corinthians 6:16-19; Ephesians 2:22).

John wrote that the son of man was in the midst of the churches and their problems (Revelation 1:12, 13; *lampstands* refers to churches, see Revelation 1:20). It is comforting to know that Jesus is not detached from us or operating by remote control. If He is the head of His body, the church (Ephesians 1:22, 23), He is in some measure experiencing what we are experiencing.

Who Are You, Lord?

John's description of our Lord is essential for us to remember as we face rough times:

1. He is royalty—"dressed in a robe reaching down to his feet" (Revelation 1:13). He is still the only ruler, "the King of kings, and Lord of lords" (Revelation 19:16).

2. He is pure—"His head and hair were white like wool" (Revelation 1:14). White is the symbol of purity, so we can trust Jesus as we wait for Him to return. He is not a politician who says one thing and means another. We can believe what He says.

3. He sees everything—"his eyes were like blazing fire" (Revelation 1:14). He is like a human flame thrower. No one is pulling wool over His eyes, for He burns the wool right off. Don't think for a moment that those who give Christians a tough time are getting by with it. Our Lord is among us and sees it all. At the proper time He will correct all that is wrong.

4. He is stable—"His feet were like bronze glowing in a furnace" (Revelation 1:15). Bronze is a very tough metal, especially when it is thoroughly refined in a furnace. The feet like bronze suggest that our Lord has not moved an inch; He is there to stay.

5. His word is powerful—"His voice was like the sound of rushing waters" (Revelation 1:15). Rushing waters can produce power that can energize, but rushing waters can also destroy in a devastating flood. Jesus' words do both. They provide energy for the Christian who feeds on them, and they will destroy those who reject them: "There is a judge for the one who rejects me and does not accept my words; that very word which I spoke will condemn him at the last day" (John 12:48).

6. He is in complete control—"In his right hand he held seven stars, and out of his mouth came a sharp double-edged sword" (Revelation 1:16). He controls the angels or messengers of His churches. (Stars are their symbols, see verse 20.) A sword can both protect and

destroy, and our Lord's sword does both. It protects the Christians and will destroy the forces of evil.

7. He is eternal—"I am the Living One; I was dead, and behold I am alive for ever and ever!" (Revelation 1:18). There is much in the environment of our period that is designed to turn our eyes away from Jesus. But He rose from the dead, and to have our lives in Him is to be in the victory circle. Just look around. Everything is dying and decaying. Only God (Jesus) is eternal.

8. He has the keys to man's destiny—"And I hold the keys of death and Hades" (Revelation 1:18). A key is used to open and to shut. "Salvation is found in no one else, for there is no other name under heaven given to men by which we must be saved" (Acts 4:12). Jesus declared, "I am the way and the truth and the life. No one comes to the Father except through me" (John 14:6).

This is quite a magnificent picture to keep in front of us while it seems as if the world is falling apart all around us. The time of waiting for the second coming is not easy. We are pulled on every side to get off the track. People, philosophies, systems, and vocations are calling for our allegiance. There is no way that we can resist the pull except by keeping our eyes on Jesus. This is what John was saying to his readers in Revelation and what the writer of Hebrews was saying to his audience:

> Let us fix our eyes on Jesus, the author and perfecter of our faith, who for the joy set before him endured the cross, scorning its shame, and sat down at the right hand of the throne of God. Consider him who endured such opposition from sinful men, so that you will not grow weary and lose heart (Hebrews 12:2, 3).

We must wait for the second coming, having Heaven's perspective and knowing that God is still on His throne (Revelation 4:1-3). He is the "Lord God Almighty, who was, and is, and is to come" (Revelation 4:8). He is worthy "to receive glory and honor and power" (Revelation 4:11).

While life around us may threaten us and try to distract us as we wait for Jesus to return, let's not allow that to happen.

Turn your eyes upon Jesus,
Look full in His wonderful face;
And the things of earth will grow strangely dim
In the light of His glory and grace.

And as we look upon Jesus, we will sing, "To him who sits on the throne and to the Lamb be praise and honor and glory and power for ever and ever" (Revelation 5:13).

A Look Within

I live right in the middle of what they call "tornado alley" of the United States. When a furious storm is raging and the tornado siren sounds, people in this area take cover. It is quite common to see them watching anxiously at the windows when the thunder sounds and the wind picks up speed, because they know what may develop.

Wouldn't it be a tragedy if someone were so enamored with the storm outside that he didn't notice that a fire had started inside his own house? Watching the clouds swirl by, seeing the lightning flash, and hearing the peals of thunder, he might keep his eyes glued to the threat on the outside and fail to notice the spreading fire within his walls. Unhurt by the storm outside, he might be burned to death because he failed to see the danger on the inside.

This type of tragedy can happen with the church. While waiting for the second coming, people can be troubled by all the perversions, persecution, tragedies, and threats to Christianity that are alive and active outside the church. They can get so anxious about these outside problems that they fail to notice the erosion going on inside the church. We must be aware that the inner problems can hurt us more than the outer ones.

While the early Christians were concerned with the threats raging against them from the outside, John reminded them to look up to see God as He is (Revelation 1). Then he immediately encouraged them to look within (Revelation 2, 3).

Inside Problems

In this chapter we will discuss some of the inner problems that John warned the church about. She needed to look within and make some changes before the return of Jesus. Five of the seven churches that John mentioned in the book of Revelation had inner problems that needed attention. Those problems are as up-to-date as the evening news.

1. *The workaholic church* (Revelation 2:1-7). The church at Ephesus was known for its deeds, hard work and perserverance (2:2). The word *deeds* refers to activities that were actually getting accomplished. *Hard work* refers to the fatiguing nature of the activities—the church members actually got worn out. They were not lazy and did not shy away from tough jobs. The word *perserverance* refers to their stick-to-it-ive-ness when the going got rough. They were not quitters. The Ephesus church also got an A+ for sound doctrine. No one could lure them off course with fancy oratory. They did not follow the theological fads of the day (2:2, 3).

So what could have been their problem? They lacked the proper motivation. Jesus said, "You have forsaken your first love" (2:4). If we are not careful, it is easy to get movements started for the right motives and keep them going long after the motivation has ceased. That can happen in any relationship. For instance, does a wife wash her husband's clothes with the same motivation she did the week after the honeymoon? Does the husband bring home the paycheck with the same motivation that he used to? It is possible to coast along and function mechanically (without thought or meaning) in a marriage.

The bride of Christ can also function mechanically, but to do so is a major threat to her well-being. In fact, if the proper motivation does not return, she may someday cease to be a church (2:5). All of us need to ask *why* we give, attend the worship service, read the Bible, or teach a Sunday-school class. Do we serve out of love or out of habit? Just keeping busy is not enough. Without the proper motives, our movements can turn into monuments that mark death as clearly as the monuments in the cemetery.

2. *The shifting sand church* (2:12-17). The church at Pergamum was located at the center of emperor worship in the province. Christians were commanded to bow down before "Satan's throne," but they refused to do so. Instead, they remained true to Jesus as their Lord (2:12, 13).

However, their curiosity about worldly practices caused them to shift a bit. They listened to teachings that weakened their morality, and some started living with the "liberal morality" as their guide (2:14, 15).

In a day when X-rated movies are popular, when sex and violence are an everyday occurrence in the media, when honesty seems never to be the best policy in business or politics, it is easy to slip into thinking that the loosening of morals is okay. Yet Jesus made clear to the people in this church that they must tighten up their morality before He returns. He has the message for us today.

Our teaching and preaching must make clear what sin is, so the members of the church will not know the world's view only. Along with Jesus and John, Paul made clear that we must clean up our lives as we wait for Jesus to return:

For the grace of God that brings salvation has appeared to all men. It teaches us to say "No" to ungodliness and worldly passions, and to live self-controlled, upright and godly lives in this present age, while we wait for the blessed hope—the glorious appearing of our great God and Savior, Jesus Christ, who gave himself for us to redeem us from all wickedness and to purify for himself a people that are his very own, eager to do what is good (Titus 2:11-14).

3. *The overly tolerant church* (Revelation 2:18-29). The church at Thyatira had deeds, service, and stick-to-it-ive-ness to their credit. Not only that, they also had the proper motives behind their activities—love and faith (2:18, 19). Yet with all this good on their side, they were too tolerant. We are not only to love what God loves, but we are to also hate what God hates (Romans 12:9).

Thyatira was a major business center filled with all kinds of guilds. A person could not easily succeed in the community unless he belonged to a guild that corresponded to his business or trade. But the guild meetings included pagan practices and acts of immorality.

The woman teacher of this church may have had good intentions behind her teaching that Christians may be engaged in "sexual immorality and the eating of food sacrificed to idols." These were common activities that took place at the guild meetings. Her point may have been that we should be involved in the mainstream of the community so that we can influence it for Christ. We must touch our culture as "salt" and "light." We cannot do that if we stand aloof. Such may have been the teaching of "that woman Jezebel."

This kind of teaching sounds logical and right. All through history it has caused many Christians to do what they should not have done. And when anyone is asked about it, the rationalizations begin: "I need to penetrate the culture, to be involved with the people around me. If I am not one of them, they won't listen to me." Penetration and involvement are mandates for Christians, but they are not accomplished within God's will by compromising our moral standards. Paul said it this way:

> Do not be yoked together with unbelievers. For what do righteousness and wickedness have in common? Or what fellowship can light have with darkness? What harmony is there between Christ and Belial? What does a believer have in common with an unbeliever? What agreement is there between the temple of God and idols? For we are the temple of the living God. As God has said: "I will live with them and walk among them, and I will be their God, and they will be my people" (2 Corinthians 6:15-16).

Paul was not saying that we are not to have any association with non-believers, for he said earlier that we must associate with them (1 Corinthians 5:9, 10). He was emphasizing that we are not to participate in their immoral activities. We must not act in agreement with their sin when we are with them. We must not be their partners in immorality.

Christians in all walks of life need to reread Jesus' words to this church at Thyatira and realize that too much tolerance is not good. We must quit compromising on moral issues before Jesus returns.

4. *The big-name church* (Revelation 3:1-6). The church at Sardis had the reputation of being a fantastically alive church, but God was not duped by their public relations propaganda. He knew they were "dead" (3:1). Chances are that at one time the church's reputation squared with what she was. But it is one thing to have a great history, and quite another to live in the present relying on that history.

Individual Christians sometimes do that. They may have been active and alive in the past. They may have built a reputation among the brotherhood—then continued to live off that reputation the rest of their lives. I have known some PhD's who haven't done a thing since they received their degrees. We must all be careful when our good reputations become occasions for pride. Pride is often what triggers a fall.

The church at Sardis was similar to the city of Sardis. Twice the city fell to outside invaders because the citizens were so "secure" that they did not watch carefully. The church in this city needed to wake up. Her members were living with a siesta-type mentality. They thought their past accomplishments assured them of a blessing when Jesus would return. But Jesus will return as a thief and will notice our present activities and attitudes, not just our past (3:3).

5. *The church of the blahs* (Revelation 3:14-22). The church of Laodicea was the church of the status quo. She was as peaceful as a cemetery. She did not get enthusiastic for anything (hot), nor did she get enthusiastic against anything (cold). She had the philosophy "whatever will be, will be" (lukewarm). That attitude makes the Lord sick (3:15, 16).

God expects the community to know where the church in that community stands. The community cannot know what the church is for or against unless the members know what they are for or against and are vocal about it. The church is not some kind of institution that is apart from us. The church is made up of all of us—God's children. What we do as individuals is what the church does.

The Hope

All of these churches were waiting for Jesus to return. It would be easy for us to be quite negative about them. Just look at the problems they had: no motivation, sexual immorality, participating in pagan worship, living loose morally, living off a past reputation, listening to false teachers, and taking no stand on the current issues. All of these were bad.

But Jesus did not send His letters about these problems to be negative or pessimistic. He wanted each situation to be changed and forgiven. Jesus realized that people are in different stages of spiritual maturity. Some are babies and live like it. Some are more mature, but at times revert to infantile behavior. Jesus does not want to lock us up in our past sins or failures. He wants to help pick up the broken pieces of our lives and help mold them into a beautiful mosaic—much like a stained glass window made up of jagged and irregular pieces that when put together become beautiful prisms as the sunlight shines through.

Jesus said the churches that did not change before His coming would face condemnation, but those that did repent and change would be blessed. What is involved in that changing? Jesus said they should remember what they had going for them, repent from their wrong activities, restore their lives to doing God's will, be faithful unto death, not fear the suffering, wake up, strengthen what they had, liven up what was dying, hold on to what was good, be pure, and overcome evil. And that is what we must do as we await His return.

As we look within, may we not be sucked into pessimism by the situations and problems. May we not give up in despair. With Jesus we can overcome the problems within and without. We must realize that two of the churches that Jesus wrote to in Revelation were very definitely accentuating the positive while waiting for Jesus' return. These two were the church in Smyrna and the one in Philadelphia.

1. *The lowly servant church* (Revelation 2:8-11). This would be a good name for the church at Smyrna. This church had tasted of life's problems (afflictions and poverty). The word for poverty is the strongest Greek word for having nothing. The church must have had no property, no building, no paid staff, no bank account, and no buses. The church was being continuously slandered by those who claimed to be religiously correct.

Yet in the midst of all this, Jesus said, "You are rich" (2:9—Read also Matthew 20:26-28). The Smyrna church evidently lived to serve God by serving others. She did not evaluate her status or spirituality by her accumulation of goods, but by her sacrificial living for the benefit of others. She was probably poor because she gave so much of herself. What a way to await the second coming!

2. *The church of grabbed opportunities.* This aptly describes the church at Philadelphia, for she took advantage of "open doors" (Revelation 3:7-13). People of that church had "little strength," yet a little was enough when coupled with God's Word, acknowledging Jesus, and taking advantage of possible opportunities. Jesus had no disappointments with that church.

How about us? Are we serving others instead of thinking of ourselves? Are we looking for open doors of opportunity? And are we ready to grab each opportunity for Jesus? Opportunities come on tiptoes and with wings. They can fly past us quickly. We must be alert and ready to grab them.

Jesus is coming back, and we are waiting. As Jesus delays His return, may we not be found lacking. May we instead be overcoming by being alert, repenting of our faults, accentuating the positive, remaining firm on the truth of God, serving others, grabbing opportunities, and "hanging in there" as the going gets rough. May we remember Paul's words:

No, in all these things we are more than conquerors through him who loved us. For I am convinced that neither death nor life, neither angels nor demons, neither the present nor the future, nor any powers, neither height nor depth, nor anything else in all creation, will be able to separate us from the love of God that is in Christ Jesus our Lord (Romans 8:37-39).

A LOOK AHEAD

As we wait for Jesus to return we live in the midst of an environment that is often anti-Christian. God asks us not only to look up (Revelation 1) and to look within (Revelation 2, 3), but also to look ahead. He wants us to see what is in store for us. He wants us to know that it is worth the waiting. He pictures a goal for us. Goals give us hope and motivate us to act to reach those goals.

Peter talked about goals and hope: "In his great mercy he has given us new birth into a living hope . . ." (1 Peter 1:3). A living hope is one that acts because it is connected to some real evidence. A girl who is engaged will plan her wedding. She has a living hope. An expectant mother will plan for the new birth. She has a living hope. A college student who anticipates graduation will do his assignments. He has a living hope. The Christian who wants to become like Christ when He returns will start becoming like him now (1 John 3:3). That is living hope.

God inspired John to help the Christians look ahead so they could wait with a living hope. John gives a bit of that look ahead at the close of every letter to the seven churches (Revelation 2:7, 10, 17, 26-28; 3:5, 12, 20, 21, which we considered in chapter 9). But as we study Revelation further, we find an even clearer and more detailed description of what is in store for us.

What Heaven Will Be Like

Heaven will be like a *perfect marriage feast*. "I saw the Holy City, the new Jerusalem, coming down out of heaven from God, prepared as a bride beautifully dressed for her husband" (Revelation 21:2). This verse presents the picture of the ceremonial union of Christ and His bride, the church—the beginning of the wedding banquet (Matthew 22:1-14).

What a day of rejoicing that will be! "Let us rejoice and be glad and give him glory! For the wedding of the Lamb has come, and his bride has made herself ready" (Revelation 19:7). That wedding banquet is going to be a fantastic one. It won't be like many wedding receptions that we have today with a little cup of punch and a small square of cake. His feast will be a celebration *par excellence*.

Heaven will have the *perfect Presence* in it. "Now the dwelling of God is with men, and he will live with them. They will be his people, and God himself will be with them and be their God" (Revelation 21:3; see also 22:4).

Heaven will be the *perfect world*. The new world will not be against us but for us. "He will wipe every tear from their eyes. There will be no more death or mourning or crying or pain, for the old order of things has passed away" (Revelation 21:4).

Heaven will have the *perfect mate*. The glorified church will be "the wife of the Lamb" (Revelation 21:9). Jesus will never neglect us, take us for granted, or mistreat us. Pure love will reign. Because of this love, we will be eternally happy.

Heaven will provide the *perfect protection*. "It had a great, high wall with twelve gates, and with twelve angels at the gates . . . There were three gates on the east, three on the north, three on the south, and three on the west" (Revelation 21:12, 13). Walls and gates are for protection. We will not have to worry about outside threats when we are in Heaven. We will have eternal security.

Heaven will be comprised of the *perfect crowd*. All of God's people will be there, including the "twelve tribes of Israel" and the "twelve apostles" (Revelation 21:12-14). What a family!

Heaven will be the *perfect place*. Heaven is described in the most magnificent of human terms (Revelation 21:15-21). Great, wonderful, and flawless beauty will saturate Heaven.

Heaven has the *perfect access*. The temple will not be there because we will not need any temporary access to God—"because the Lord God Almighty and the Lamb are its temple" (Revelation 21:22). We will have immediate and personal access to God. What an opportunity!

Heaven will have *perfect illumination*. The sun and moon will not be needed, "for the glory of God gives it light" (21:23; 22:5).

In Heaven will be the *perfect response*. There will be no hint of rebellion there—"The nations will walk by its light, and the kings of the earth will bring their splendor into it" (Revelation 21:24). No one will try to usurp the authority of God. There will be no competition there, and no one will have to "lock up" at night to have a sound sleep (Revelation 21:25, 26).

In Heaven will be *perfect ecology*. "Nothing impure will ever enter it, nor will anyone who does what is shameful or deceitful, but only those whose names are written in the Lamb's book of life" (Revelation 21:27).

The *perfect resources* in Heaven will result in *perfect health*. The water of life is as clear as crystal, and the fruit and leaves of the tree of life keep health and prevent any curse (Revelation 22:1-3).

Heaven has the *perfect blessing:*

Behold, I am coming soon! My reward is with me, and I will give to everyone according to what he has done. I am the Alpha and the Omega, the First and the Last, the Beginning and the End. Blessed are those who wash their robes, that they may have the right to the tree of life and may go through the gates into the city (Revelation 22:12-14).

Conclusion

What great things are ahead for us! But if we really want that kind of future, we must be living properly now. If we want to participate in the marriage feast, we need to identify ourselves with Jesus now. If we want to be in God's presence in Heaven, we need to allow Him to live in us now. If we want to live in the perfect world, we need to be influencing our world for the better now. If we want to have an eternity of protection, we must allow God to be our refuge now and express our trust in His will and way. If we want access to God in Heaven, we need to approach Him now.

If we want perfect illumination, we need to walk in the light of His Word now. If we want to have the perfect response then, we must practice obedience now. If we want to live in purity then, we must be more pure now. If we want to partake of perfect health then, we need to take advantage of God's resources available to us now. If we want the perfect blessing then, we need to live as blessings now.

In short, if we want to live in Heaven, we must first accept His invitation now. "The Spirit and the bride say, 'Come!' And let him who hears say, 'Come!' Whoever is thirsty, let him come; and whoever wishes, let him take the free gift of the water of life" (Revelation 22:17).

Just accepting the invitation is not enough. "Since we live by the Spirit, let us keep in step with the Spirit" (Galatians 5:25). The Spirit is God's deposit with us that guarantees our inheritance until the redemption of those who are God's possession (Ephesians 1:13, 14). The word *deposit* was used to refer to the first payment of the whole price. It was also used to refer to an engagement ring.

In the Holy Spirit, God has given us a foretaste of Heavenly living. So if we want to live in Heaven with the characteristics that will be there, we must allow the fruit of the Spirit to multiply and be expressed in our lives on earth. To live with "love, joy, peace, patience, kindness, goodness, faithfulness, gentleness, and self-control" (Galatians 5:22, 23) is the way to wait for the return of Jesus. That brings a bit of Heaven to earth.

We do not know when Jesus will return, but we can know how and why. We can know also how we are to live and wait for Him.

Jesus is coming soon! While we wait and live for Him, may "the grace of the Lord Jesus be with God's people" (Revelation 22:21).

OTHER BOOKS BY KNOFEL STATON

Spiritual Gifts for Christians Today

Paraphrase of the Declaration and Address

The Gospel According to Paul

Don't Divorce the Holy Spirit

Home Can Be a Happy Place

The Perfect Balance

The Servant's Call

You Don't Have to Stay the Way You Are

Struggle for Freedom

Grow, Christian, Grow!

Discovering My Gifts for Service

How to Know the Will of God

How to Understand the Bible

Check Your Lifestyle

Check Your Character

Meet Jesus

Thirteen Lessons of First, Second, and Third John

Check Your Discipleship

P. 22
John
Wesley
Qude
(Prepared)